A PENNSYLVANIAN IN BLUE

The Civil War Diary of Thomas Beck Walton

Edited by

ROBERT A. TAYLOR

Burd Street Press

This Burd Street Press publication
was printed by
Beidel Printing House, Inc.
63 West Burd Street
Shippensburg, PA 17257 USA

In respect for the scholarship contained herein, the acid-free paper used in this book meets the guidelines for permanence and durability of the Committee on Production Guidelines for Book Longevity of the Council on Library Resources.

For a complete list of available publications
please write
Burd Street Press
Division of White Mane Publishing Company, Inc.
P.O. Box 152
Shippensburg, PA 17257 USA

Library of Congress Cataloging-in-Publication Data

Walton, Thomas Beck, 1840-1913.
   A Pennsylvanian in blue : the Civil War diary of Thomas Beck Walton / edited by Robert A. Taylor.
      p.   cm. – – (Civil War heritage series ; v. 6)
   Includes bibliographical references.
   ISBN 0-942597-82-6 (softcover : alk. paper)
   1. Walton, Thomas Beck, 1840-1913– –Diaries.   2. United States. Army. Pennsylvania Infantry Regiment, 195th (1864-1865)   3. United States– –History– –Civil War, 1861-1865– –Personal narratives.
   4. Pennsylvania– –History– –Civil War, 1861-1865– –Personal narratives.
   5. Soldiers– –Pennsylvania– –Lancaster County– –Diaries.   6. Lancaster County (Pa.)– –Biography.   I. Taylor, Robert A., 1958-   .
   II. Title.   III. Series.
   E527.5 195th.W35 1995
   973.7'444–dc20   95-18341
                                                               CIP

PRINTED IN THE UNITED STATES OF AMERICA

Table of Contents

Introduction

"I, Thomas B. Walton enlisted in the service of the United States [with the] 195th Regiment Company H on the 2nd day of March 1865 for the term of one year." Thus begins the diary of one of the over 300,000 Pennsylvanians who answered their country's call and served in the Union armies during the Civil War. Walton's experiences as recorded in his pocket journal were neither unique or unusual, but they do chronicle what the struggle between the states was like for one ordinary soldier and his peers. While escaping the bloody horrors of the battlefield, Walton and his comrades in arms underwent all the other trials and discomforts of being common soldiers in the long struggle.

Thomas Beck Walton was born on August 10, 1840 near New Holland in York County, Pennsylvania. He was one of five sons born to Hiram and Mary Dunkel Walton, both originally from Chester County. The Waltons were a farming family, so young Thomas and his brothers grew up in a rural setting near the banks of the Susquehanna River. When Thomas reached adulthood he chose not to remain on the land but to seek a trade. He eventually left New Holland for Middletown where he learned the shoemaker's craft.[1]

The coming of civil war in 1861 altered the lives of the Walton family, as it did so many others. The firing on Fort Sumter, combined with the Union's defeat at the battle of Bull Run in July, fueled the desire of farmers' sons and shop clerks across Pennsylvania as well as the rest of the country to enlist and be part of what many believed to be a short, glorious adventure. By early September, two of Hiram Walton's children, Amos George and Hiram Frank, joined Company B, 45th Pennsylvania Volunteer Infantry. By the end of the year they and their regiment would be garrisoning far-off Otter Island near the mouth of the North Edisto River off the coast of South Carolina.[2]

Thomas Walton, on the other hand, decided not to enlist immediately. Letters from his brothers probably convinced him that soldiering far from home was anything but adventurous, so he remained behind. However, by 1862 his thoughts were on other things besides his cobbler's trade. By the end of that year he married Emma Nopsker of Bainbridge, Conoy Township, Lancaster County, the nineteen-year-old daughter of a fairly prosperous local laborer. The young couple began their new life amid the uncertainties of their time.[3]

Despite such joyous occasions, the grim realities of the war then raging continued to be brought back to those at home. The 45th Pennsylvania, returned from the Carolina coast, saw heavy fighting at South Mountain on September 14, 1862. After a charge against a Confederate position across an open field, the 45th counted twenty-one of its men killed, including Private Amos George Walton. He and the others lost in the battle were wrapped in their blankets and gently buried on the field with a crude headboard marking each grave. The Walton family now fully understood how high the price for preserving the Union would be.[4]

The war's cost loomed large to all the residents of southern Pennsylvania by the summer of 1863 when General Robert E. Lee's Army of Northern Virginia marched deep into the state in a campaign that resulted in the bloody three-day clash at Gettysburg. The home front in the Keystone State now became the front lines with civilians encountering scores of Confederate troops. Lieutenant General Jubal Early's command advanced into York County, up to the banks of the broad Susquehanna, threatening the state capital to the north. As Johnny Rebs gave Confederate scrip for items taken from local stores, they told unhappy merchants that their currency was "better than your greenbacks, as we are on our way to Harrisburg, Philadelphia and New York, and the war will soon be over."[5] Such boasting proved premature, but Pennsylvanians in the region touched by the Southern invasion never enjoyed the same sense of security again.

Such anxiety was not baseless, as future events unfolded. As in 1863, the summer of 1864 was a time of crisis. Another Confederate force, again led by "Old Jube" Early, slipped up the Shenandoah Valley with the goal of relieving some of the pressure Grant and the Army of the Potomac were applying to Lee's men in Virginia. By the second week of July grey-clad troops even entered the District of Columbia. Later that month Confederate cavalry under Brigadier General John McClausland raided Pennsylvania and all but destroyed the town of Chambersburg. Such actions proved that this cruel war was far from over, and much blood and treasure need yet be spent to achieve victory.

The Walton family received another bitter shock at roughly the same time Early's invasion was taking shape. Private Hiram Frank Walton was killed in action while serving with his regiment on June 30, 1864 at the battle of Cold Harbor. Frank Walton had continued soldiering with the 45th Pennsylvania after the death of his brother in 1862 in Kentucky, Tennessee, Mississippi, and finally back in Virginia. But the now veteran private opted not to reenlist for another three years like the bulk of his comrades. While preparing to attack at Cold Harbor he remarked to a fellow soldier that he "did not feel like going into this engagement." Friends tried to persuade him to hang back when the fighting began since he had only a few days left to serve and nothing to prove to them. Walton however rejected their advice, believing that it would reflect badly on him if he did not participate, then went into battle with his company. The 45th Pennsylvania advanced into "a murderous fire" of rifle bullets and canister, and Private Frank Walton was one of 45 men lost to the 45th Pennsylvania by the end of the day.[6]

With such losses and the South nowhere near beaten, calls went out for even more Pennsylvanians to volunteer for the army that summer. Governor Andrew Curtin announced authorization to raise a number of new regiments for a term of one hundred days. One of these, the 195th Pennsylvania Volunteer Infantry, was recruited largely in Lancaster County. Men joined based on many different reasons: patriotism, concern about being conscripted into the service, and the promise of considerable bounty money. New recruits reported to Camp Curtin near Harrisburg, where the 195th was officially organized on July 24, 1864.[7]

This regiment was fortunate to have an experienced officer picked to be its commander. Colonel Joseph W. Fisher, a native of Lancaster County since 1840, rose from a tailor's apprentice to become a lawyer and a Republican state politician by 1860. After the outbreak of war he was elected a captain in the 5th Pennsylvania Reserves, but by the Second Battle of Bull Run, he led it as its colonel. Fisher and the 5th saw action from South Mountain and Antietam to Gettysburg and Mine Run in 1863. By the middle of that year he received a brigade command and led it through the beginning of Grant's Virginia campaign. Fisher decided to return home in 1864, probably due to poor health, where he expected to stay. But Governor Curtin's call led him to once again take the field at the head of the new 195th.[8]

Almost immediately after its creation the new regiment moved to Baltimore and then on to Monocacy Junction to guard the important railroad bridge and rail lines located there. For two months the 195th pulled this vital, though less than exciting, duty. The 860-odd members of the regiment were trained during this period in the skills of the soldier and spent time on the drill field, but with only one hundred days to serve, such instruction and general discipline surely suffered.

During its last month of duty, the 195th Pennsylvania shifted westward into Berkley County, West Virginia to defend the Baltimore and Ohio Railroad as far as Hedgesville. Headquartered at North Mountain Station, soldiers of the 195th performed general picket service until the expiration of their term on October 20. Losing such a number of troops posed a real problem for the local Union command, so every effort was made to entice as many men as possible to reenlist for a term of at least one year. Colonel Fisher used his political talents to persuade some three hundred members of the 195th to sign up for another tour, while the rest eventually mustered out at Camp Curtin early in November. The re-enlistees formed a three-company battalion under the temporary command of Captain Henry D. Markley.[9]

In February, 1865 Governor Curtin requested that Fisher remain in command of the 195th and begin the raising of seven new companies to bring it up to full regimental strength. Canvassing for the new volunteers centered in Lancaster County, with nine companies of the new 195th being composed primarily of Lancaster men. Only Company A was different, being predominantly made up of soldiers from neighboring Berks County. One of those choosing to step forward and enlist was twenty-four-year-old Thomas B. Walton.[10]

Why did he decide to enter the army at this time? Walton left no clue in his diary, but several factors no doubt influenced him. One surely was the shadow of being drafted, and its accompanying stigma. Another was the fact that the 195th was a one-year regiment, and the war seemed unlikely to last that long. Financial considerations probably loomed large; each one-year volunteer receiving a one hundred dollar enlistment bonus. Next, his brother Joseph had already decided to sign up, so Walton would not have to serve completely alone. Lastly, the memory of his two slain brothers could not have been too far from his mind. Perhaps Walton felt compelled to finish the job they had started.

Thomas Walton enlisted in Lancaster on March 2, after the usual processing. Military clerks took down his vital statistics and a brief physical description: eyes grey, hair light colored, complexion fair, height five feet three and one half inches. Surgeon John Atleeh examined the prospective recruit and certified that he was "free from all bodily defects and mental infirmity, which would in any way disqualify him from performing the duties of a soldier." Finally he would be officially sworn into Federal service by enrolling officer Captain Thaddeus Stevens, nephew of the powerful Republican congressional leader. Walton then began an eight-day furlough to get his affairs in order before actually leaving to join his regiment.[11]

Now the new Private Walton was introduced to the rough life of the Civil War soldier at Camp Cadwalader in Philadelphia, and then transported by rail to the 195th's bivouac near Martinsburg, West Virginia where the new version of the regiment was organized on March 16, 1865. Soon after arrival he and his fellows in Company H began learning the skills of the soldier and the rhythms of military life. Colonel Fisher set the tone with his first general order to his new command, telling his men that they "must obey all orders of their officers and strive to become acquainted with the duties pertaining to their present calling."[12] Walton appears to have had little difficulty in adjusting to camp life, which roughly followed this schedule:

Reveille	6:00 AM
Breakfast	7:00 AM
Sick Call	7:30 AM

1st Sergeants Call	7:45 AM
Guard Mount	8:00 AM
Fatigue Call	8:00 AM
Squad Drill	8:30-9:00 AM
Company Drill	10:00-11:00 AM
Drummers' Call	12:00 noon
Battalion Drill	3:00-4:00 PM
1st Sergeants Call	4:30 PM
Dress Parade	5:00 PM
Company Drill	5:30-6:00 PM
Tattoo	8:30
Taps	9:00 PM[13]

The 195th's first area of operations would be at the northern end of the Shenandoah Valley, with the general mission of picketing the fords of the Shenandoah River to prevent Confederate raiders like Colonel John S. Mosby from striking Federal posts on the Baltimore and Ohio Railroad. Walton and his fellow soldiers knew that simple guard duty anywhere in what was known as "Mosby's Confederacy" was not without its dangers. An attack could come at any time from any direction, making the men especially vigilant and uneasy.[14]

When Lee's battered army surrendered at Appomattox Court House in April, Walton and the rest of the 195th were doing garrison duty in the town of Berryville. Walton recorded that this "very good news" reached camp on a rainy April 10, 1865. Cannons soon boomed in celebration and spirits among the men soared, sure that their army days were now numbered. This joyous mood evaporated quickly when word of President Abraham Lincoln's assassination arrived in the Valley. Walton wrote in his diary of rumors and faint hopes that Lincoln survived his head wound and "had come to his sences." But the grievous truth finally sank in and Walton and the rest went on with their duties, unsure of what each day would now bring.

On June 6, the 195th Pennsylvania received orders to march southward up the Valley, passing through towns like Winchester and New Market made famous during the war. Most of the 195th pitched its tents at Harrisonburg, with lucky Walton being assigned to provost marshal duty in the town itself. While never expressing any animosity toward Southerners, Walton did note in his journal the less than enthusiastic way the citizens of Harrisonburg celebrated the first Fourth of July after the end of the war. Even these people, however, soon began the process of reconciliation by the middle of the month, with Walton and other provost guards supervising the taking of the oath of allegiance and the first post-bellum election in the vicinity. Such activities marked the real beginning of the Reconstruction era in the former Confederate states.

Walton's diary tells a story of soldier life in the Union army that touches on many of the themes common to that experience. He endured hard marches, exposure to the elements, monotonous and at times short rations, unpopular officers, and the problems of discipline. Officers in the 195th had a growing difficulty keeping their men in line as many, knowing the war to be over, thought they would soon be discharged like the dozens of veteran regiments mustering out almost daily. Such was not to be the case, however. With the realization that exit from the army would not be coming soon, desertions began to occur at an alarming rate. Some eight men deserted from Walton's Company H in June alone (see Appendix II). On July 24, he even wrote about the threat that his fellow soldiers might break two men out of the regimental guard house, a sign of major dissatisfaction.

Discipline grew even more problematic when the regiment was ordered to Washington, D.C. on August 1, 1865. Few Washingtonians probably paid much attention as yet another blue-clad unit tramped up Pennsylvania Avenue upon its arrival, interest waning with the passing of the Union armies in the earlier Grand Reviews. After settling into camp near Georgetown, the 195th learned that its new duties would entail guarding government property and general provost service around the city. The War Department made it clear that the 195th had enlisted for a one-year term and would serve the same before any thought of mustering it out. Bad feelings built up between officers and enlisted men until insubordination broke out in Company I and a corporal "spoke very rough," as Walton put it to Colonel Fisher. During the rest of the 195th Pennsylvania's tour, its leaders remained hard pressed to maintain order in the unit. Even Walton eventually was placed on report for being partially out of uniform while on guard duty on August 14.

Generally Walton enjoyed his stay in the nation's capital. His duties were none too taxing and he had plenty of time to see the sights of the busy city. Walton wandered through the Capitol building, saw the displays at the Patent Office, and walked among the exhibits of the Smithsonian Institution. Food was mostly good and plentiful, barracks housing adequate, and mail from home fairly constant. However, while Walton's morale appeared solid, that of the rest of Company H steadily declined. Each passing day in Washington brought home the fact that there would be no early discharges. As a result the number of men deserting grew larger as the fall and winter of 1865 approached.

While in Washington Walton also had the chance to see a bit of history and rub shoulders with at least one famous figure of the day. On October 7, while standing guard at the railroad depot, he saw none other than Lieutenant General Ulysses S. Grant pass through the station. Later in November he attended the execution of Captain Henry Wirtz at the Old Capitol Prison for his role as commander of the infamous Andersonville prison in Georgia. The hanging of Wirtz seemingly made little impression on Walton, for he spent the rest of the day touring the Smithsonian.

Interestingly the last significant formal military task performed by the 195th Pennsylvania Volunteer Infantry would be the conducting of a military funeral for a later regular army brevet lieutenant colonel named Colbridge on January 27, 1866. Four days later the regiment officially left federal service, and by February 2 Walton was back at Camp Cadwalader to pick up his "buzzard," which was Civil War soldier slang for discharge papers. On the next day the ex-Private Walton happily made his way home back to Bainbridge. For him, the Civil War was indeed finally over.[15]

Walton began the task of beginning civilian life again with the girl he left behind, his wife Emma. He returned to shoemaking and made an adequate living until health problems forced him to leave Bainbridge and move north to Atkinson's Mills in Mifflin County. By 1879 his family again moved to Huntingdon, where Walton entered business as a merchant. Here he became a well-known citizen, joined the First Baptist Church of Huntingdon, and raised his two sons. Walton earned a reputation among his friends and neighbors as "a good man in every way – a real Christian gentleman."[16]

Like so many others, Thomas Walton never forgot his service during the war, and with the passing of years desired the company of other veterans who once wore the blue uniform. In 1883 he joined the George Simpson Post No. 44, Grand Army of the Republic, and remained an active member for the next thirty years. Recapturing the past was not without some pain, for his two lost brothers never really left his memory. In 1912 he made a sentimental journey to the national cemetery at Antietam and finally located the grave of his brother Amos George, since moved from its interment site on South Mountain. Walton had tried previously to find the exact spot, but was never able to place it before. The fear that he might lay among the unknown dead was now finally gone.

Thomas Beck Walton turned seventy-three the next year, and occupied himself with his business and the G.A.R. In January, 1913 he was elected Senior Vice Commander of the George Simpson Post, with an elaborate banquet to mark the occasion. Unfortunately by November his health further deteriorated and at last his heart failed. Death came quietly to the old soldier in his Huntingdon home early on the morning of November 28, 1913. With his family and Grand Army of the Republic comrades gathered he was laid to rest in the local Riverview Cemetery three days later.[17]

Editorial Note and Acknowledgments

One of the things Private Thomas B. Walton shared with his fellow Civil War soldiers was an at times cavalier attitude to the rules of grammar and spelling in his writing. Walton himself was a poor and inconsistent speller, as well as indifferent to capital letters and punctuation such as periods. His prose was typical of Union and Confederate diarists in that his entries are for the most part composed of run-on sentences. In such cases editors are greatly tempted to correct such writings to the point where their original authors would be unable to identify it as their own work. However, doing nothing to aid the modern reader in understanding what they are reading is unacceptable as well.

In preparing Walton's journal, hopefully an editorial balance has been struck between both extremes. Punctuation and capital letters have been added where needed, and run-on sentences spliced into more meaningful ones. Names of individuals and geographical locations have also been corrected, but those misspelled words that the reader can understand are left as they appeared in the original diary. Only those difficult to understand are fixed and marked with brackets, as are all other editorial intrusions. Walton's diary has been left as close to what he wrote in 1865 as possible in order to let him speak in his own way with his own words.

As with all such projects, the editor owes debts to many people and institutions without whose help this work could never have been completed. First and foremost thanks must go to Mrs. Judy Squires of Fort Pierce, Florida, a descendant of Thomas Beck Walton and current owner of his diary. She made its editing possible and labored many hours on its initial transcription. Mr. Charles F. Faust of Shillington, Pennsylvania, a Civil War scholar, generously shared his voluminous notes on members of the 195th Pennsylvania Infantry. Librarians and archivists at the following institutions made major contributions: The United States Army Military History Institute at Carlisle, Pennsylvania; the National Archives and the Library of Congress in Washington, D.C.; the Indian River County Public Library in Vero Beach, Florida, and the Indian River Community College library in Fort Pierce, Florida. Lastly special thanks must go to Dr. Lewis N. Wynne of the Florida Historical Society for showing me how rewarding the discovery and editing of Civil War soldier diaries can be; and to Mr. and Mrs. George R. Taylor for aid above and beyond the call of duty; and to Dr. Ann McMullian for her considerable support and friendship during this endeavor. The photograph which Walton had taken of himself and mentioned in the text could not be located.

Fort Pierce, Florida
Robert A. Taylor

The Civil War Diary of Thomas Beck Walton

I, Thomas B. Walton enlisted in the service of the United States [with the] 195th [Pennsylvania Infantry] Regiment on the 2nd day of March 1865 for the term of one year. Returned home in the evening of the same day with a furlow of 8 days exspiring on the 10th day of said month.

Thursday, March 9, 1865 –

Evening [at] 5 o clock started for Lancaster. Stayed at the Black Horse Hotel overnight.

Friday, March 10 –

Morning. Took breckfast at the hotel at 7 o clock and reported at the Marchal['s] office. And then marched to the railroad then left for Philadelphia at half past 10 o clock. Arrived at west Philadelphia at one o clock then marched 4^1/$_2$ miles to Camp Cadwalader Barricks No. 2.[1] Got a good bunk with [Private] Rudy Lewis and [Private] Zack Garrett.

Satterday, March 11 –

Arose in the morning very well. Got to writing a letter home [and] sent if off. Took breckfast – plenty to eat. All day stayed in Barrick until about 7 o clock in the evening then taken in front of Barricks No. 4. Kept us standing until 9 o clock then was run into Barrick. Found no bunk [and] laid on the flore with [Private] Henry King and [Private] J[ohn] S. Kauffman. Rested pretty well but much crowded.

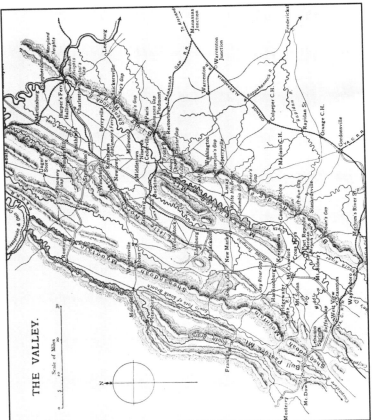

The Shenandoah Valley during the Civil War
(from G. F. R. Henderson, *Stonewall Jackson and the American Civil War*, 1936 edition)

Sabbath, March 12 –

Morning – very well. Spent part of the time in reading the testement but spent rather a rough sabbath. And then in the afternoon we were called up for one days rachions and then paid off in the evening. Then about ten o clock we took the [railroad] cars for Baltimore.

Monday, March 13 –

Arrived at Baltimore about ten and half o clock. Got dinner then laid on the pavement until about three o clock then took the cars for Harpers Ferry. Great cheering by the citizens as we pass along the road. Got to Harpers Ferry about 10 o clock at night [and] was taken in to quarters in a church. The town is in a valley [with] hills on both sides.

Tuesday, March 14 –

Morning. Arose after sun up [and] feel very well. Got part of a good nights rest. Sent a letter home with 3 dol[lars] and 33 cents [and] sent 30 dollars by Adams Express. Got fotograph taken here in a wagon. Left Harpers Ferry at half past three [and] landed at Martinsburg at half past five. Marched to Camp about half [a] mile [and] struck tents in the evening. Messed with [Privates] Rudy Lewis, Len Engle, Andrew Elles, Joseph Markley, [Sergeant] Emanual Demmy, and my self.

Wensday, March 15 –

Had a good nights rest – the first since left home. Feel very well this morning. Rained part of the night – this morning still raining. Very disagreeable in Camp. Our Capt. [Joseph Styer] and second Leuit. [Jefferson S. Galbraith] came to camp this afternoon.[2] Got my bible which was very acceptable.

Thursday, March 16 –

Morning – feel very well. Was formed in line – not organized yet. Very stormy this morning. Sent a letter to wife [and] had dress parade at 4 o clock. Raining again this evening [and] still very stormy. Rained in the tent [and] had disagreeable night.

Friday, March 17 –

Morning – fell very well. Very cold and disagreeable. [Commenced] building a new tent. Had company and squad drill this evening.

Satterday, March 18 –

Rested very well last night. Feel very well. Started this morning about 2 miles to the woods for logs to build a tent. Returned to camp about noon [and commenced] building the tent. Got it ready to move in this evening.

Sabbath, March 19 –

Morning – feel very well. Had Regimental inspection this morning. Met [Corporal] J[oseph] K. Walton in camp sick. Wrote a letter to my wife. Had dress parade a 4 o clock [and] roll call at 8 o clock.

Monday, March 20 –

Morning – very well. Roll call at six o clock [and] drill at 8 o clock. Finished our tent [then] had regimental drill at 3 to 4 o clock. Roll at 8 in the evening.

Tuesday, March 21 –

Morning – very well. Roll call at 6 o clock and drill daily in the forenoon. Cleaning at the Col.['s] tent [then] regimental drill from 3 to 4 o clock. Raining and stormy all night. Drawed our guns.[3]

Wensday, March 22 –

Morning – very well but very cold and stormy all day. Was in the woods for logs for cook house in the afternoon. Sent a letter to wife.

Thursday, March 23 –

Very well but very cold and stormy all night. Very cold and stormy all day. Was in the woods guarding team. General Inspection this afternoon.[4]

Friday, March 24 –

Feel very well but very cold. Snowed last night. Started out on Picket at nine o clock w/[with Private] John Weaver.

Satterday, March 25 –

Releaved at 7 o clock from Picket. Very cold all night. Got to Camp about 8 o clock [and] found the regiment ready to march. Fell in rank [and] started for Charlestown Va. Distance about 23 miles. Very tired when got to camp. Arrived 6 o clock [and] pitched tent w/[with Private] B[enjamin] Minich and Brother Joseph.

Sabbath, March 26 –

Feel very well, but pretty cold last night. This morning General Inspection. Pitched our tents over again [then] dress parade at 6 o clock in the evening. Very cold all day. Received a letter from wife and photographs [with] 2 [news]papers. Wrote a letter to wife.

Monday, March 27 –

Morning – feel very well. Got the cold a little. Out 3 hours on skuad drill this afternoon. This afternoon drill 1½ hours and then sent to the woods for wood for the cooks.

Tuesday, March 28 –

Morning – very well. Not so cold last night. The orders is for roll call in the moring [and forming] in line of battle at 6 o clock. Drill at 9 to 12 afternoon [then] 2 to 5 [PM]. Roll call at 8 in the evening.

Wensday, March 29 –

Morning very well. Whether very pleasant [but] was routed out at 1 o clock last night in line of battle expecting an attack by [Colonel John S.] Mosby.[5] Had dress parade this afternoon and inspection.

Thursday, March 30 –

Morning – caught a slight cold. Did not feel very well this morning. Picket firing kept up all night [and] was drawn in line of battle twice. Laid on our arms all night. Rained pretty mean all day [but] drilled a short time in the afternoon. Received a letter from wife [and] also sent one home.

Friday, March 31 –

Feel pretty well this morning. Rained the grater part of the night. North[ward] a heavy gust rained in our tent [and] got our feet wet. Drilled part of the forenoon [but] rained pretty near all day. Three regiments here today – 2 yesterday.[6] Drawed 20 rounds of cartridges this evening [with] orders for the Regt. to go on Picket tommorow morning.

Satterday, April 1 –

Morning – got up early [and] felt very well. Drawed four days rashons [then] fell in line ready for a march about 8 o clock. Martch about 10 miles to a small village called Cabletown [which] goes by the name Little Masechusets – an old delapidated place. Was taken on guard at the Bull Skin Creek. 6 of us on one post stood about 2 hours during the night.

Sabbath, April 2 –

Morning – fell very well. On picket at the Bull Skin Creek. Stood 2 hours during the day [and was] releaved at 4 o clock. Went to camp [and] wrote a letter to send to wife. Went to bed about 8 o clock. Orders to be ready to fall out at a moments warning.

Monday, April 3 –

Morning – feel pretty well but got up with a slight cold. Pack[ed] up about 10 o clock to martch back to Charlestown. Left a quarter past one o clock [and] arived about 4 o clock in Camp. Pitched tents in another field. After we was through we was drawn in line and the dispatch was read to us that our army was in Richmond for which our 9 harty cheers was given. Cheering all through the camp [and] 30 shots was fired [by] artillery in Charlestown.[7]

Tuesday, April 4 –

Morning – feel very well. Aroused very erley and orders to get ready for martch. Recev'd a letter from my wife, [then] left camp about 10 o clock. Marched out the Winchester Pike about one mile [and] halted about half past one o clock. Then started [again] – marched very hard. Got to Berryville about 8 o clock very tired. Thought we would encamp thare but still went on about 3 miles further. The majority of the Company stopt to rest along the road. Got to where the Regt. had stopt about 11 o clock [with] I and B[enjamin] having the tent pitched. The distance from Charlestown to Berryville [was] 12 miles [with] marching a distance of 15 miles.

Wensday, April 5 –

Got up very well. Placed my knapsack on a wagon [but] hardly got time to make coffee. Was marched rite off past along Winchester [Pike]. About noon halted a little while – got me time to make coffee. [Then] marched on to Stevensons Station, a distance of about 10 miles. Went into camp about $2^{1}/_{2}$ o clock [and] pitched tents but very tired. Had a hard march.

Thursday, April 6 –

Morning – arose not very well. Got the cold. Raining this morning [and] very disagreeable. Sent a letter to wife. received a letter from wife [and] one from David [C. Walton].[8] Cleared off this afternoon. Ordered on dress parade at 6 o clock [and heard] dispatch that [General Robert E.] Lee is surrounded.

Friday, April 7 –

Morning – pretty cool. Moved our tents in line [and] was on a commity to collect money to buy officers swords. Dress parade at six o clock. Order to have our shoes black when on duty – some of the boys was put to the rear on account of having dirty shoes. A dispatch read from Winchester that [General Philip H.] Sheridan has whipt Lee.[9]

Satterday, April 8 –

Morning – feel very well. Was out on drill this forenoon [and] this afternoon ordered to clean up. A beautiful day. Wrote a letter to G. A. Leauman. Dress parade at six o clock [then] was at meeting at the Christian Commission.[10]

Sabbath, April 9 –

Morning – feel very well. Got ready for inspection at 9 o clock. Wrote a letter to wife also 1 to George. Was at preaching at 3 o clock [then] dress [parade] at six o clock.

Monday, April 10 –

Morning – very well. but wether very disagreeable – raining. Had very good news this morning that Lee surrendered his whole army. 50 guns fired at Winchester in honor of the grate victory [and] 20 guns fired near here this afternoon. 100 guns fired at Winchester. This afternoon was at the general headquarters doing fatague duty.[11]

Tuesday, April 11 –

Not very well – [weather] still very disagreeable – wet and muddy. Drawed a pair of shoes. [size] nines [and] traded in another company for sixes. Nothing transpiring during the day [but] drill this afternoon.

Wensday, April 12 –

Morning – very well. Out on drill this forenoon. Sent a box to F[rederick] M. Gramm with 16 pair of boots.[12] Cleared off at noon [and] regimental drill this after noon. [Commenced] raining again. Wrote a letter to wife [then] dress parade this evening. Rained all night.

Thursday, April 13 –

Very well this morning. Put on target firing. Cleared off today [with] the mud drying up again. Regimental drill this afternoon. News very [encouraging] – draft postponed – very fine day.

Satterday, April 15 –

Morning – very well but raining again and very disagreeable. Orders to pack up ready for a march at eleven o clock. All ready to start [and] the [railroad] cars backed up. Ready about a quarter of eleven [when] the orders were again counter manded.[13] News came to camp that President Lincoln was killed – shot in the head.

Sabbath, April 16 –

Morning – feel very well. Was out on inspection this morning. Received a letter from wife also wrote one to wife. News that Lincoln is not dead [and] that he has come to his sences again.[14] Out of rashions – nothing to eat but what we buy.

Monday, April 17 –

Morning – feel very well. Was on general review about 2 miles from camp [and] out on dress parade this evening. No rashions yet. Wrote a letter this after noon in the Christian Commission to F. R. Brenner.[15]

Tuesday, April 18 –

Morning – feel very well. Was detailed to go on picket [but] traded with [Private Isaac] Sensenig for camp guard. My post at the Col.['s] headquarters.

Wensday, April 19 –

Morning – very well. Came off guard at nine o clock. No drilling today on account of the funeral of the President. Our chaplain [Issac E. Graeff] preached at ten o clock in [an orchard] close to camp

Colonel Joseph W. Fisher, 195th Pennsylvania Volunteer Infantry
(Courtesy Gil Barrett Collection, USAMHI)

[and] Col. [Joseph W.] Fisher also spoke. We had dress parade in the evening. Wrote to wife [and] also received a letter from wife.

Thursday, April 20 –

Fell very well this morning. Routed out at about half past one o clock [with] orders to get ready for a march at half [past] three. Left camp about half past five [and] went down to the railroad. Laid thare until eight o clock [and] then we was marched to our own camp again. Orders to fix up our quarters again. All the rest of the regiments from around us left to go to Summit Point. Thare was other regiments [that] came [to] releive us. No drilling this afternoon.

Friday, April 21 –

Morning – feel very well. Got up at 4 o clock [and] cooked our brakfast. Started at 6 o clock [and] marched very easy – rested every hour. Got to Summit Point about twelve o clock [and] went into camp whare another regiment had left. Got to cleaning up. Distance from Stevenson['s Station] to Summit Point about 12 miles. Pitched our tents in the afternoon [and] seen Wm. McFeeters.[16] Rained a small shower during the night.

Satterday, April 22 –

Morning – very well. Was all engaged in policing the streets [with] no drill today. Drawed gun slings and different [accouterments]. Ran out of rashions [but] got an order from the Capt. for ham and potato[es]. Was detailed for fatague duty [and] hauled a load of wood for the Col.

Sabbath, April 23 –

Morning – very well. Company Inspection. Out of provisions – drawed more this evening [then] dress parade. Very cold all day – wrote a letter to wife.[17]

Monday, April 24 –

Morning – feel very well. Was out on Company drill in the fore noon [and] regimental drill in the after noon. Dress parade in the evening [with] orders to have roll call five times a day.

Tuesday, April 25 –

Morning – feeling very well. Went out on Company drill. Called in and [then] went out target practicing in the fore noon.[18] In the after noon had regimental drill [and] dress parade in the evening.

Wensday, April 26 –

Morning – very well. Orders to get ready for inspection. I was detailed for fatague while inspection was going on. Regimental drill this afternoon [and] dress parade this evening. Received a letter from K. M. Galso [and] also from A. R. B.

Thursday, April 27 –

Morning – very well. Was detailed for picket duty. Left camp at $\frac{1}{2}$ past seven [and] got to the picket line at 10 o clock. Stood eight hours out of 24. Sent a letter to wife [and] also received 2 letters from wife. Out of rations.

Friday, April 28 –

Morning – very well. Got to camp off of picket at eleven o clock. Got some more rations when we got to camp. Was at the creek [and] took a good wash – also washed my clothes. Did not drill on the afternoon [but] was out on dress parade. Got a letter from G. A. L[eauman].

Satterday, April 29 –

Morning – feel very well. Very pleasant morning – no drill today. Got time to wash [then] good news. We was all taken in front of the Col.['s] tent. A dispatch [was] read that [General Joseph E.] Johns[t]on surrendered – [then] give nine hardy cheers.[19] Raind this after noon [and] no dress parade this evening. Rec[eived] a letter from wife.

Sabbath, April 30 –

Morning – very well. Very fine day – was mustered for pay this morning then inspection. Then we was called up to give our names for white gloves. This noon [Private] Andrew Elles shot himself in the leg [and] was taken to Hospital. Dress parade this evening [and] drawed more rations.

Monday, May 1 –

Feel very well this morning. Was out on Company drill [and] raind a while in the morning but just before noon. Regimental drill in afternoon [but] no dress parade this evening.

Tuesday, May 2 –

Morning – very well. Wether very pleasant. Got ready to go out to drill [but] was ordered back and got ready for review. Dress parade this evening.

Wensday, May 3 –

Morning – very well. Was on water detail. The regiment had inspection [and] an order read that our own regiment had the praise of being well drilled and a fine looking set of men. Also that our General [Green B. Raum] resigned.[20]

Thursday, May 4 –

Morning – very well. Detailed for Camp guard. Our Regt. out on general inspection – inspected guns and knapsacks. Drawed our white gloves [and] the regt. had them on on dress parade. Sent a letter to wife today.

Friday, May 5 –

Morning – very well. Got off guard nine o clock. Regimental drill in the afternoon. Dress parade in the evening – marched twice around the camp.

Satterday, May 6 –

Morning – very well. Rained last night [but] cleared off. Had no drill today [which] gave us time to wash. Dress parade in the evening and marched around camp.

Sabbath, May 7 –

Morning – very well. Packed up ready to go on General review. Started at eleven o clock [and] returned at 3 o clock. Had an election to see which one of the officers was to have the sword. [Second Lieutenant] J[efferson] G[albraith] had 26 votes – [First Lieutenant] J[ohn] R[odgers] 6 – [Captain] J[oseph] S[tyer] 2 but there is yet a difficulty to be settled. Wrote a letter to wife.

Monday, May 8 –

Morning – very well. Was out on Company drill in the forenoon and out on regimental drill in the afternoon. Just got to camp when it [commenced] raining. No parade. Wrote a letter to G. M. Beane [and] received two from wife. One that had been written on the 10th of April [and] came around by Washington and one dated on the 5th of May.

Tuesday, May 9 –

Morning – very well. Raining all day off on on. No drill of any kind. I was detached to help to have rations [brought] from the [commissary]. No dress parade. Wrote a letter to J. R. Brenner.

Wensday, May 10 –

Morning – very well. Was detailed for Camp guard but got on the patrol guard. Only had to stand 2 hours that was after night. Rained very hard but slept in the bunk all night.

Thursday, May 11 –

Morning – very well. Was releaved off guard at nine o clock. Thare was inspection ordered but put it off. Went for regimental drill this afternoon but when we got to the railroad we was ordered back on double quick on account of a gust coming up. After we got to our quarters it commesnt raining [and] raining ever since. Wrote a letter to wife.

Friday, May 12 –

Morning – very well. Had general inpection about 12 o clock by Gen. [Thomas H.] Neill.[21] Regimental drill in the afternoon and dres parade in the evening.

Satterday, May 13 –

Morning – very well. A very fine morning. Was out target practicing in the fore noon [and] regimental drill in the afternoon. Dress parade in the late evening. An order [was] read giving our regiment the praise of [being] the best regiment that Gen[eral] Neill inspected.

Sabbath, May 14 –

Morning – very well. Company inspection in the forenoon. Went to the woods in the afternoon and wrote a letter to wife. Dress parade in the evening.

Monday, May 15 –

Morning – very well. Company drill in the forenoon [and] Brigade drill in the afternoon. Very warm. Received a letter from wife.

Tuesday, May 16 –

Morning – very well. Was detailed for picket [but] traded with [Private] J[ohn] Weaver for Camp guard. Got to [go] on 2nd relief. A very warm day.

Wensday, May 17 –

Morning – very well. Got releaved at nine o clock. Very warm again today. Then inspection this forenoon but the Col. gave out. Had regimental drill but it was very warm. Dress parade this evening.

Thursday, May 18 –

Morning – very well. Very pleasant morning. [Private] H[am] Ney and myself made a sink at the cook house. The regiment commesnst making a hardour over the camp. A very heavy rain came up about dress parade time. Got the diarrhea this evening. Sent a letter to wife.[22]

Friday, May 19 –

Morning – not well. Still got the diarrhea. Done nothing all day but it was wet all day and no drill. Got a letter from wife.

Satterday, May 20 –

Morning – not well. Still got the diarrhea but not quite so bad. No drill today. Rained in the afternoon a couple of showers.

Sabbath, May 21 –

Morning – not very well. Rained all day very hard [but] the regiment had dress parade in the evening. Still off duty.

Monday, May 22 –

Morning – still not well – off duty. Wrote a letter and sent it home with [Private] Joseph Markley. The regt. had inspection in the forenoon and regimental drill in the afternoon. [Private] C[hristian] Hoover and myself was seting in the woods pretty near all day. The regt. came in early off of drill [because] we got orders to pack up ready for a march. Left camp after dark in the evening. I got my knapsack in a wagon and rode in an ambulance myself. Got close to Berryville about one o clock [and] laid down in the field and the wet grass.

Tuesday, May 23 –

Morning – feel pretty well [but] only got the diarrhea worse again. Encampt close to town close to a woods [at] a very pleasant place. The distance from Summit Point to Berryville about eight miles. No drilling today but dress parade. Still off duty.

Wensday, May 24 –

Morning – still getting better but off duty yet. No drill all day but dress parade in the evening.

Thursday, May 25 –

Morning – feel pretty well. Did not report to the doctor today [though] not on duty.[23] Sent a letter to wife also one to G. D. Company drill in the forenoon [and] an election held in town. Dress parade in the evening. One of our guards fired at last night.

Friday, May 26 –

Morning – feel pretty well. Whether very disagreeable. Rained pretty near all night and all day. No drilling all day. No news [but] got a letter from wife.

Satterday, May 27 –

Morning – feel very well. No drilling all day. Cleared off [then] dress parade in the evening.

Sabbath, May 28 –

Morning – don't fell very well. I was at the doctor['s] this morning but I am taking meadcine that I got from a doctor in the band.[24] Dress parade this evening [and] sent a letter to wife.

Monday, May 29 –

Morning – do not feel very well. Reported to the doctor [and was] excused from drill. Thare was company drill in the forenoon [and] regimental in the afternoon. Dress parade in the evening.

Tuesday, May 30 –

Feel pretty well this morning. Inspection this morning at nine o clock. We was taken out for regimental drill but ordered back for a general inspection at half past 3 o clock. But [instead] passed off with dress parade. Wrote a letter to wife.

Wensday, May 31 –

Morning feel pretty well again. Had inspection at nine o clock. Was ready to go out on regimental drill at half past five but it was pased off with dress parade. Got a letter and dry beef and onions that was sent with Markley from my wife.

Thursday, June 1 –

Do not feel very well. Got the diarrhea back worse again. Thare was nothing done all day but preaching in the woods at 10 o clock. [Lieutenant] Col. [William L.] Bear made a speech in the evening.[25] Wrote a letter to wife.

Friday, June 2 –

Morning – feel a little better but was not on duty. No drill in the forenoon. Regimental drill in the afternoon [and] dress parade in the evening.

Satterday, June 3 –

Feel very well this morning. No drill this being wash day. Dress parade in the evening. Wrote a letter to B. Bowers [and] recev'd a letter from wife [with $] 5.00 in[side].

Sabbath, June 4 –

Morning – very well – went on duty. Had company inspection in the morning [and] dress parade in the evening. Wrote a letter to wife [then] had orders to prepare for a martch.

Monday, June 5 –

Morning – very well. Was out washing in the forenoon [and] had regimental drill in the afternoon. Very hot – several fell over. Dress parade in the evening.

Tuesday, June 6 –

Very well this morning. Went on guard on third releaf. There was no drill in forenoon [and] regimental drill in the afternoon. About 4 o clock got orders to march [and] the guard was taken off. Got ready [then] was sent to guard the Sutler. Marched to Winchester [and] got there at about 1 o clock at night. Left about six [PM] – distance about 12 miles.

Wensday, June 7 –

Morning – feel very well. Laying here for further orders. Left Winchester about noon [and] left old Companys behind.[26] Marched about 10 miles towards Staunton [and] passed several towns – one by the name of New Town [and] Kernstown & Milltown.

Thursday, June 8 –

Morning – feel very well. Left about 4 o clock – very warm. Passed through Middletown Next was Strawsburg [Strasburg]– a distance of about 12 miles from Winchester. Next was Mirrortown [Maurertown].[27] Marched near to woods. [Wood]stocks a distance of 18 miles from Strawsburg. Marched a distance of about 17 miles whare we encamped for the night.

Friday, June 9 –

Morning – feel very well. Left about 4½ [o clock and] passed through Woodstock. Next was Edonburg [Edenburg] [which] we passed about 9 o clock. Next was Hawkentown [Hawkinstown]– a very old place.[28] Got to the Shannendoah about 12 o clock whare we took dinner. Then started in the rain along the river through Mt. Jackson to the fording whare we crossed the river, and encamped for the night– distance about 14 miles.

Satterday, June 10 –

Morning– very well. Got up at 4 o clock. Ready to start at 5 [and] marched on. Passed one town by the name of New Market – a prety large place. Got short of rations. The distance of today['']s march was 21½ miles.

Sabbath, June 11 –

Morning – fell very well. Got up [and] took breakfast on short rations. Marched about 1½ miles to Harrisonburg. Passed through about 1 mile whare we encamped 4 companys of us. 3 companys went on to Staunton with [the] 192nd Pennsylvania Infantry] regt. [and] 12th [Pennsylvania] cavelry.[29] We have a pleasant place here [and] can go to town any time. [Private] C[alvin] G[arreth] and myself went to town and got bread and butter. No camp guard. Wrote a letter to wife.

Monday, June 12 –

Morning – very well. Went to the run and washed all my clothing & mended in afternoon. Had no drill all day.

Tuesday, June 13 –

Morning – very well. Moved camp over to a woods [then] was detailed to go to Harrisonburg for provost duty. 11 out of our company [are] quartered in the lower story of the Mason's lodge. Very nice place – got good bunks. Receieved a letter from wife.

Wensday, June 14 –

Morning – very well. Was on guard at the offace of the provost Marchals. 6 of us only stood [guard] one hour at a time. Wrote a letter to wife.

Thursday, June 15 –

Morning – very well. Moved our quarters on the second story [to] a nice room. Nothing to do all day [and] was out in the country for cherrys.[30]

Friday, June 16 –

Morning – very well. Nothing to do all day. Was in camp in the morning after rations – a very fine day.

Satterday, June 17 –

Morning – very well. Nothing to do all day. Was after cherrys this forenoon & into camp this evening for rations.

Sabbath, June 18 –

Morning – very well. Was on patrole today in camp. At noon got a letter from B. Bowers.

Monday, June 19 –

Morning – very well. Drawed our rations here at our quarters. Had nothing to do all day [and] wrote a letter to wife.

Tuesday, June 20 –

Morning – very well. Nothing to do all day.

Lt. Colonel William L. Bear, 195th Pennsylvania Volunteer Infantry
(Courtesy Gil Barrett Collection, USAMHI)

Wensday, June 21 –

Morning – very well. Was on guard at the provost offace – a very fine day.

Thursday, June 22 –

Morning – very well. Was releaved at 8 o clock [and] went to camp to see the boys. Nothing to do all day but run about.

Friday, June 23 –

Morning – very well. Nothing to do all day. Recev'd a letter from wife [and] also wrote home. Nothing transpired today worthy of note.

Satterday, June 24 –

Morning – very well. On patrole today on third releaf – only on at 5 o clock. A very pleasant day [and] nothing transpired of note.

Sabbath, June 25 –

Morning – very well. Had inspection this morning at our quarters [then] went to camp to pass the time. [A] fine day.

Monday, June 26 –

Morning – very well. Was in camp to draw our beef [then Corporal] Rudy [Lewis] & myself cooked it. Was in the country this afternoon [and it] rained a smart shower [but] cleared off nice. [Private Samuel] A[ble] & [Private Henry] Seachrist deserted today.

Tuesday, June 27 –

Morning – very well. Was on patrole first releaf. Capt. J[oseph] Styer got his discharge today but did not leave today. Nothing transpired.

Wensday, June 28 –

Morning – very well. Nothing to do today. The sick that was left at Winchester came today. News that we must leave here but not credited.

Thursday, June 29 –

Morning – very well. Nothing to do today. Recev'd a letter from wife [and] also sent one home. [Lieutenant] Col. Bear went home on furlow. Good news from home – one year men all to be discharged.

Friday, June 30 –

Morning – very well. Nothing to do all day. Went on guard in the evening at the comasary. Our rations came from Staunton.

Satterday, July 1 –

Morning – very well. [First Sergeant] Issaac Filbert and [Private] F. Fettenberger went home on furlow [and] started urly. Capt. Styer also left for home with his discharge.[31] Got releaved from guard at six o clock [and it] rained a very hard shower. Drawed our clothing this evening.

Sabbath, July 2 –

Morning – very well. Had general inspection at 9 o clock. Wrote a letter to wife [and] was in camp today.

Monday, July 3 –

Morning – very well. Had no duty today so I cooked the meat [and] traded [the] lard for bread.

Tuesday, July 4, 1865 –

Morning – very well. On second releaf of patrole. Our batalion from camp had a parade through town this evening [and] not one flag out in the whole town. The citizens had a picknick at Bridgewater.[32] Had another parade through town in the evening [and] all had candles on thar guns. Thay had the headquarters illuminated. We also had our quarters and the Marchals offace [with] nine candles at each window.

Wensday, July 5 –

Morning – very well. Nothing to do today [and] was in camp. A very warm day [and] nothing transpired worthy of note.

Thursday, July 6 –

Morning – very well. Nothing to do today. Signed our clothing bill for this month [and] Col. Fisher went to Winchester this morning. A very warm day.

Friday, July 7 –

Morning – very well. Was on guard at the [Provost] marchal[']s offace. No news today.

Satterday, July 8 –

Morning – very well. Nothing to do today. Was in camp and also washed my clothes.

Sabbath, July 9 –

Morning – very well. Had inspection at 7$\frac{1}{2}$ o clock by the major [Henry D. Markley].[33] Was in the country for blackberrys. Went to hear a darkey preacher in the afternoon [and] had a good shower of rain.

Monday, July 10 –

Morning – very well. Inspection today. Nothing transpiring worthy of note.

Tuesday, July 11 –

Morning – very well. Was in camp for the meal [and] done the cooking. Was in the country for berrys. This afternoon the cavelry came down from Staunton on thare way to Winchester [and] stopt here over night.

Wensday, July 12 –

Morning – very well. Raining. The cavelry started early on thare way. [It is] supposed they are to be discharged.[34] All kind of reports about going to Winchester. Wrote a letter to wife and one to F[rederick] M. Gramm.

Thursday, July 13 –

Morning – very well. On guard today at the store. Sun very warm [though] cool this evening. Nothing transpiring worthy of note [and] no mail this evening.

Friday, July 14 –

Morning – very well. Very cool this morning to last night. Got off guard at 8 o clock [then] was out about a mile in the country to a horse rase.

Satterday, July 15 –

Morning – very well. Nothing to do all day [and] nothing transpired of importance.

Sabbath, July 16 –

Morning – very well. Was on patrole today [on] third releaf. Was in camp this morning [and] nothing transpired today.

Monday, July 17 –

Very well. Nothing to do today. Business very brisk in the [Provost] offace with country folks in taking the oath preparing for the election.[35]

Tuesday, July 18 –

Morning – very well. Done the cooking. A very busey day [since] the election came off very quick. [First Sergeant] Issaac Filbert and [Private] F. Feltenberger came back today with a letter from wife and 5.00 dollars in[side].

Wensday, July 19 –

Morning – very well. Was on third patrol today [and] wrote a letter to wife. [Sergeant] J[oseph] Bachman went him on a French furlow.[36]

Thursday, July 20 –

Morning – very well. Nothing to do all day [and] no news.

Friday, July 21 –

Morning – very well. Nothing to do all day but very warm. No news.

Satterday, July 22 –

Morning – very well. Nothing transpired worthy of note.

Sabbath, July 23 –

Morning – very well. Was on guard at the store [and] wrote a letter to wife.

Monday, July 24 –

Morning – very well [but] very warm. Nothing to do today but out guarding the prisson till 12 o clock at night. It was [threatened] to be broken open by the company to get out prissoners J.M. and A.B.[37]

Tuesday, July 25 –

Morning – very well. Nothing to do today. 3 days rations came down from Staunton.

Wensday, July 26 –

Morning – very well. On patrole today. Orders to pack up for a march [and] left about 3¹/₂ o clock. Marched about 6 miles [and] laid over for the night.

Thursday, July 27 –

Morning – very well. Left at 5 o clock [then] marched about 19 miles until noon. Passed through New Market [and] eat dinner at the north branch of the Shanendoah. Laid over until 3 o clock then marched six miles and laid over for the night. Passed through Mount Jackson to Hawkentown [Hawkinstown]. A very hard march [and] very warm.

Friday, July 28 –

Morning – very well [though] feet very sore. Started at 5 o clock [and] passed through Edenburg and Woodstock. Laid over at 11 o clock for dinner [then] started again at 2 o clock. A very warm day [and] one died of Co. G.[38] Distance of the days march 21 miles – a hard march. Laid over at 9 o clock at night.

Satterday, July 29 –

Morning – very well. Started at 5 o clock [and] got to Winchester about a quarter past 3 o clock. Laid at the end of town a short time then marched through and laid over for the night. 19 miles about the distance of our march today. It went pretty well – only my feet very sore. Recev'd a letter from wife.

Sabbath, July 30 –

Morning – very well. Very cool last night. Started to Stevenson[']s Station at 4 o clock. Laid with a tent [due to] a very heavy dew [and my] gum blanket get wet through. Got a letter from wife. Distance [today] 5 miles.

Monday, July 31 –

Morning – very well. Wrote a letter to wife [then] left Stevenson['s Station] at 3 o clock. Got to Harpers Ferry at 3 o clock [and] laid over until 8. Distance 32 miles. Left then for Washington [but] could not see much of the country after night. Had freight cars [and] slept pretty near all night.

Tuesday, August 1 –

Morning – very well. Got to Washington about 6$^1/_2$ o clock [and] was taken into a barrick. Stacked arms [and] got breakfast at 8 o clock. Distance from Harpers Ferry to Washington 103 miles. Laid in thare until after dinner then marched up Pennsylvania Avenue out about 3 miles near Georgetown. Laid thare about half an hour then was detailed to go to G Street W[h]arf for guard. Was in to see the Capatol [and] board[ed] at the Soldier[']s Retreat – very good evening.[39]

Wensday, August 2 –

Morning – very well. Nothing to do today. Wrote a letter to wife [and] was out in camp this afternoon. Detailed this evening for guard on second releaf.

Thursday, August 3 –

Morning – very well. Nothing transpired today worthy of note [and] came off guard this evening.

Friday, August 4 –

Morning – very well. Nothing to do today – very warm. Got paid four months wages $63.45 cents.

Satterday, August 5 –

Morning – very well. On guard today [and] nothing transpired worthy of note.

Sabbath, August 6 –

Morning – very well. Nothing to do this day. Wrote a leter to wife [and] go on guard this evening. Rained this evening.

Monday, August 7 –

Morning – very well. Very warm today. Got a letter from wife.

Tuesday, August 8 –

Morning – very well. Went to the city in the street cars [and] expressed 30 dollars home.[40] Went to the Capitol. Pattent office, and the Smithsonian Institute. Go on guard this evening.

Wensday, August 9 –

Morning – very well. Was down at the Navy Yard this morning – no news.

Thursday, August 10 –

Morning – very well. Nothing to do today. Recev'ed a letter from wife [and] also one from F[rederick] M. Gramm.

Satterday, August 12 –

Morning – very well. Left last night from camp: Sergt. [Abraham] T[rostel] & [Private] J[efferson] R[easer].

Sabbath, August 13 –

Morning – very well. On guard today, wrote a letter to wife also one to F[rederick] M. G[ramm].

Monday, August 14 –

Morning – very well. Had orders to prepare for inspection but had none. Had a fall out with [Sergeant Reuben G.] Sherman for not keeping [accouterments] on all day [and] was sent to camp under arrest.[41]

Tuesday, August 15 –

Morning – very well. Still under arrest but allowed to go whare we please. Nothing transpiring worthy of note.

Wensday, August 16 –

Morning – very well. Done a little work for the Col. then was released. J[ohn] H. Smith and wife [Susanna] came to see us [and] brought us a grate many things: tomatoes, onions, peaches, pies, cakes, vinegar, strawberrys in cans [and] also preserves, apple butter and eggs.[42]

Thursday, August 17 –

Morning – very well. Detailed for city guard [and] got on post at 17th Street and K [Street]. Got a letter from wife [and] also wrote one home.

Friday, August 18 –

Morning – very well. Came off guard at 9 o clock [and] went to camp. Had nothing to do all day [and] no dress parade this evening.[43]

Satterday, August 19 –

Morning – very well. Went on guard at the comassary this morning. Nothing transpiring worthy of note.

Sabbath, August 20 –

Morning – very well. Came off guard at 9 o clock. Dress parade every day [and] wrote a letter to wife.

Monday, August 21 –

Morning – very well. Went on guard at the Sanatarry Commission [and] that satisfies me about that place.

Tuesday, August 22 –

Morning – very well. Came off guard at 9 o clock. Got a pass with [Corporal Tarleton] Hal Beane to go to J[ohn] H. Smith[']s [and] had a very good diner.[44]

Wensday, August 23 –

Morning – very well. In the city on guard at the 17th and I Street[s]. Very cold during the night.

Thursday, August 24 –

Morning – very well. Came off guard at nine o clock. Got a letter from wife [and] also wrote one home.

Friday, August 25 –

Morning – very well. Went on guard at the commasary on first releaf [and] night very cold.

Satterday, August 26 –

Morning – very well. Came off guard [and] dress parade this evening.

Sabbath, August 27 –

Morning – very well. Went on guard this morning at the comasary in the city.

Monday, August 28 –

Morning – well. Came off guard [and] dress parade this evening. [Private] B[enjamin] Minich brought me a letter from home. I also wrote one home.

Tuesday, August 29 –

Morning – well. Did not get off guard today. Dress parade in the evening.

Wensday, August 30 –

Morning – well. On camp guard today [and] liken to have a rough time in camp. A corprel spoke very rough to Col. Fisher.[45]

[In the face of such defiance and declining morale, Colonel Fisher issued the following as General Order No. 10 on August 30, 1865:

The Col. commanding regrets to find a species of insubordination growing up in this command which if permitted in and allowed must result in great injury to the service.

When this Regt. was recruited and organized it was done with the clear and distinct understanding to continue for one year or during the war. The men received very large local bounties and might almost be said to have enlisted from mercenary motives. Many men of the command have deserted and strong efforts have been made and are being made to induce others to desert.

While it is desirable that we should all get to our homes and families (And none desires to do so more than the Col. commanding). Yet it is the part of a good Soldier to serve the government as long as his services are required, and that too without any grumbling.

You should bear in mind that your pay for a year including Bounty, clothing, rations, medical attendance and monthly pay is very far beyond that received by laborers and mechanics generally: besides that labor throughout the county is extremely scarce, so that tousands of men, many of them returned soldiers are out of employment. But above all your duty to your Country demands that you should await the decision of your government as to the time of your discharge, which will doubtless be before very long.

Means are now being put in operation to arrest deserters and when arrested to bring them to adequate punishment. The habit of writing to the departments must be stopped or it will receive the reward merited by disobedience, and it is hereby plainly announced that hereafter any officer, non-commissioned officer or Private who shall write or send to any department or Hd. Qrs. above Regimental, any such written communication without sending such communication through proper channels shall be punished for disobedience of orders. You were told in Genl. Order No. *One* that it was the desire of your commander to make you good and efficient Soldiers. that desire still exists. Every wish and thought is for your benefit, and comfort, and nothing has been done or will be left undone which can be done to make you comfortable, but acts of insubordination cannot, must not, and will not be allowed.

This order to be read at four (4) consecutive evening parades.][46]

Thursday, August 31 –

Morning – well. Came off guard [and] mustered for 2 months pay. Wrote a letter to wife. Ten out of Co. I refused to do duty [and] was put in the [Old] Capitol prisson.[47] [Lieutenant] Col. W[illiam] L. B[ear] made a speech on dress parade. Cap[tain Don Juan] W[allings] tried to get a cheer for them but could not raise it.[48]

Friday, September 1 –

Morning – very well. On city guard at the comassary [with] nothing transpiring.

Satterday, September 2 –

Morning – very well. Came off guard [and] dress parade this evening.

Sabbath, September 3 –

Morning – well. Went on guard this morning at the comassary in the city.

Monday, September 4 –

Morning – very well. Came off of guard this morning. Wrote a letter to wife [and] also one to F[rederick] M. Gramm.

Tuesday, September 5 –

Morning – well. Went to the comasary on guard [and] had guard mount at Brigade headquarters. Got a letter from wife.

Wensday, September 6 –

Morning – very well. Came off of guard [and] wrote a letter to wife. Dress parade this evening.

Thursday, September 7 –

Morning – very well. Went on guard at the comasary.

Friday, September 8 –

Morning – well. Came off of guard. Dress parade [with] nothing transpiring worthy of note.

Satterday, September 9 –

Morning – very well. Went on guard at the comassary again [and] wether getting a little cooler.

Sabbath, September 10 –

Morning – not well. Had the chill and fever [and] got a sevre headache this morning. Came off of guard [and] wrote a letter to wife.

Monday, September 11 –

Morning – very well. Went on guard at the comassary. No news today.

Tuesday, September 12 –

Morning – well. Came off of guard [and] recev'd letter from wife.

Wensday, September 13 –

Morning – well. Went on guard again at 17th and K Street[s].

Thursday, September 14 –

Morning – well. Came off of guard. Got a pass for [Private] J[ohn] Kauffman and myself [and] went over to J[ohn] H. Smith[']s. Wrote a letter to wife.

Friday, September 15 –

Morning – well. Went on guard at the comassary [...] No news.

Satterday, September 16 –

Morning – well. Came off of guard [and] dress parade this evening.

Sabbath. September 17 –

Morning – well. Went on guard at G Street wharf. No news.

Monday, September 18 –

Morning – well. Came off of guard. Cleaning up all day for inspection [but] none on account of the rain. Very stormy this evening. Wrote a letter to wife.

Tuesday, September 19 –

Morning – well. Had inspection about one o clock [and] went on guard at 3 o clock. Got a letter from wife.

Wensday, September 20 –

Morning – well. Came off of guard [and] dress parade in the evening.

Thursday, September 21 –

Morning – well. Went on guard at G Street wharf [then] wrote a letter to wife.

Friday, September 22 –

Morning – well. Came off of guard – no news today.

Satterday, September 23 –

Morning – well. Went on guard at the comasarry.

Sabbath, September 24 –

Morning – well. Came off of guard [and] wrote a letter to wife.

Monday, September 25 –

Morning – well. Had nothing to do today.

Tuesday, September 26 –

Morning – well. went on guard at the Paymasters General.[49] Recev'ed a letter from wife [and] also wrote one.

Wensday, September 27 –

Morning – well. Came off of guard at five o clock. Wrote a letter that was sent with [Private] C[alvin] Garreth with ten dollars.

Thursday, September 28 –

Morning – well. Went on guard at 17th & K Streets [and] nothing transpired worthy of note.

Friday, September 29 –

Morning – well. Came off of guard this morning.

Satterday, September 30 –

Morning – well. Went on guard at the G Street wharf.

Sabbath, October 1 –

Morning – well. Came off of guard [and] wrote a letter to wife. Dress parade in the evening.

Monday, October 2 –

Morning – well. Went on guard at 17th & I Streets – no news.

Tuesday, October 3 –

Morning – well. Very cold last night [then] came off of guard.

Wensday, October 4 –

Morning – well. Went on guard at 17th & I [Streets].

Thursday, October 5 –

Morning – well. Came off of guard [and] wrote a letter to wife. Got orders this afternoon to pack up [and] left camp about four o clock. Marched down to the Depot [and] went into barricks. All slept on the flore [and] eat at the mess house.

Friday, October 6 –

Morning – well. Was detailed this morning for duty in the depot – a very nice place.

Satterday, October 7 –

Morning – well. Nothing transpiring [but] seen Gen. [Ulysses S.] Grant get in the cars.[50]

Sabath, October 8 –

Morning – well. Wrote a letter to wife.

Monday, October 9 –

Morning – well. No news today.

Tuesday, October 10 –

Morning – well. No news.

Wensday, October 11 –

dito.

Thursday, October 12 –

dito.

Friday, October 13 –

Well. My furlough came at noon dated the 14th. Drawed 2 months pay – 32 dol[lars]. Left for home in the 4:30 train [and] got to Baltimore at 6 o clock. Laid until 8 [then] got to Goldsborro at 12[PM]. Went back to York Haven at 2[AM] on a freight train [and] got my uncle to take me across the [Susquehanna] river. Got home at four o clock in the morning.

Satterday, October 14 –

At home. Spent the day very pleasantly with my family and seeing some of the folks in town.

Sabbath, October 15 –

Morning – well. Spent the whole day at home.

Monday, October 16 –

Dispatch came for me to return to the regiment to be mustered out.

Tuesday, October 17 –

Started with J.H, [Private] F. F[ettenberger], [Private] J]ohn] E[bersole] [and] crossed the [Susquehanna] river. Left Wolf's Station at 9 o clock [and] got to Washington at half past five in the evening.[51] Found the boys all right.

Wednesday, October 8 –

Morning. Went on at my old post again [and] wrote a letter to wife.

Thursday, October 19 –
On duty – nothing transpiring.

Friday, October 20 –
dito.

Satterday, October 21 –
dito.

Sabbath, October 22 –
Well – wrote a letter to wife.

Monday, October 23 –
nothing transpiring.

Tuesday, October 24 –
Well. The 194th Ohio [Infantry] regiment was mustered out today.[52]

Wednsday, October 25 –
Well. Recev'd a letter from wife [and] also wrote one.

Thursday, October 26 –
Going on duty – no news.

Friday, October 27 –
dito.

Satterday, October 28 –
dito.

Sabbath, October 29 –
Wrote a letter to wife.

Monday, October 30 –
No news.

Tuesday, October 31 –
Recev'd a letter from wife.

Wednsday, November 1 –
Morning – well. Wrote a letter to wife.

Thursday, November 2 –

No news.

Friday, November 3 –

[Private] J[acob] Sides came back from furlough [and] brought me a letter from wife. Also shirt Drawers.

Satterday, November 4 –

No news.

Sabbath, November 5 –

Well.

Monday, November 6 –

Well.

Tuesday, November 7 –

Well.

Wednsday, November 8 –

Well. Got another man on my post [so] only get on every other day.

Thursday, November 9 –

Well – on duty today.

Friday, November 10 –

Well. Seen [Captain] H[enry] Wirtz hung in the forenoon.[53] In afternoon at the Smithsonian Institute.

Satterday, November 11 –

Very well.

Sabbath, November 12 –

Very well – wrote a letter to wife.

Monday, November 13 –

Very well – recev'd a letter from wife.

Tuesday, November 14 –

Very well.

Wednsday, November 15 –

Wrote a letter to wife.

Thursday, November 16 –

Very well.

Friday, November 17 –

Very well.

Satterday, November 18 –

Was at Smithsonian [and] recev'd a letter from wife.

Sabbath, November 19 –

Wrote a letter to wife.

Monday, November 20 –

Got paid off today [and] I got [$] 63.30. Sent 50 dollars with [...] money.

Wensday, November 22 –

Recev'd letter from wife [then] went home on a pass.

[Colonel Fisher issued the following to his regiment as General Order No. 11 on November 26, 1865:

> Numerous complaints having been made by the Field Officer of the Day as to the manner of performing guard duty by the men of this command.

> The Col. Commanding takes occasion to call the attention of Officers of the guard and non–Commissioned officers on duty to some of the matters complained of to show how guard duty should be performed.

> Sentinels while on post have been frequently sitting down, others smoking, reading newspapers, standing conversing with their friends and sometimes their gun resting against the wall on post.

> These things must be corrected.

> Sentinels while on post must walk their respective beats with arms carried at some position taught in the school of the Soldier. Officers entitled to salute must be saluted. No

conversation must be carried on between the sentinel on post and other person or persons.

No smoking or reading of newspapers, books, or other matter. The Officer of the day, Officer and Sergeant of the guard as well as the different Corporals will be held accountable for the correct performance of duty by the Sentinels and will see that every part of guard duty is properly attended to.

This order to be read at Guard Mount every morning until further orders.]⁵⁴

Monday, November 27 –

Morning. Bought a house. Started for the regiment at noon [and] arrived at 8 o clock.

Tuesday, November 28 –

Wrote a letter to wife.

[In the face of a wave of desertions in his regiment, Colonel Fisher issued General Order No. 46 on November 30, 1865 which stated that "no officer or enlisted man in this Command is allowed to wear any civilian clothing but appear in the proper uniform and no other."]⁵⁵

Sabbath, December 3 –

Recev'd a letter from wife [and] also wrote one.

Tuesday, December 19 –

Was sent to Kendall Green Wood yard.

Friday, January 19, 1866 –

Was releaved by the 214[th Pennsylvania Infantry regiment] and [went] back to the Company.⁵⁶

Wendsday, January 31 –

Was mustered out at about 9 o clock.⁵⁷ Left in the cars at a quarter of 8 o clock pm [and] got to Baltimore at 11 o clock.

Thursday, February 1 –

Arived in Philadelphia about 8 o clock AM [and] went to Camp Cadwalader. In the evening went to Carpenter Street to lodge.

Friday, February 2 –

Went to camp in the morning [and] got our discharge about 12 o clock. Left for home about 8 o clock PM.

Satterday, February 3 –

Arived at home about 3 o clock AM.

HAPPY [...] are we all.
Caught rabbits.

—————————————————————————— *Appendix I*

Company H, 195th Pennsylvania Infantry:
The Men

This partial roster is taken from data in the 195th Pennsylvania's regimental descriptive book in the National Archives and Samuel P. Bates' *History of the Pennsylvania Volunteers 1861-1865.*

**Captain William D. Stauffer, Company H,
195th Pennsylvania Volunteer Infantry**
(Courtesy Ronn Palm Collection, USAMHI)

Captain William Stauffer

Age: 25   Place of Birth\Residence: Lancaster, Pa.
Occupation: Clerk
Date mustered into service: August 10, 1865
Date mustered out of service: January 31, 1866

First Lieutenant John S. Rodgers

Age: 24   Place of Birth\Residence: Lancaster, Pa.
Occupation: Teacher
Date mustered into service: February 28, 1865
Promoted from private: March 13, 1865
Date mustered out of service: January 31, 1866

Second Lieutenant Jefferson G. Galbraith

Age: 24   Place of Birth\Residence: Lancaster, Pa.
Occupation: Machinist
Date mustered into service: March 16, 1865
Date mustered out of service: January 31, 1866

First Sergeant Isaac S. Filbert

Age: 22   Place of Birth\Residence: Snyder County, Pa.
Occupation: Laborer
Date mustered into service: February 28, 1865
Date mustered out of service: January 31, 1866

Sergeant Joseph Bachman

Age: 29   Place of Birth\Residence: Lancaster County, Pa.
Occupation: Boatman
Date mustered into service: February 27, 1865
Date mustered out of service: January 31, 1866

Sergeant Emanuel Demmy

Age: 25   Place of Birth\Residence: Lancaster County, Pa.
Occupation: Blacksmith
Date mustered into service: March 2, 1865
Date mustered out of service: January 31, 1866

Sergeant Reuben G. Sherman

Age: 37   Place of Birth\Residence: Berks County, Pa.
Occupation: Painter
Date mustered into service: March 9, 1865
Deserted November 16, 1865

Corporal Tarleton Bean

Age: 24   Place of Birth\Residence: Washington County,
            Maryland: Lancaster County, Pa.
Occupation: Farmer
Date mustered into service: March 2, 1865
Date mustered out of service: January 31, 1866

Corporal Randolph (Rudy) F. Lewis

Age: 25   Place of Birth\Residence: York County, Pa.
Occupation: Boatman
Date mustered into service: March 3, 1865
Date mustered out of service: January 31, 1866

Corporal Joseph Walton

Age: 26   Place of Birth\Residence: York County, Pa.
Occupation: Distiller
Date mustered into service: March 1, 1865
Date mustered out of service: January 31, 1866

Private Samuel K. Able

Age: 27   Place of Birth\Residence: York County, Pa.
Occupation: Laborer
Date mustered into service: March 3, 1865
Deserted June 29, 1865

Private Andrew Elles

Age: 19   Place of Birth\Residence: Snyder County, Pa.
Occupation: Cabinetmaker
Date mustered into service: March 3, 1865
Discharged by General Order on May 25, 1865

Private Levi L. Engle

Age: 28   Place of Birth\Residence: Lancaster County, Pa.
Occupation: Gardener
Date mustered into service: March 3, 1865
Date mustered out of service: January 31, 1866

Private F. Fettenberger

Age: 29   Place of Birth\Residence: York County, Pa.
Occupation: Laborer
Date mustered into service: March 2, 1865
Date mustered out of service: January 31, 1866

Private Calvin Garreth
Age: 42   Place of Birth\Residence: Adams County, Pa.
Occupation: Laborer
Date mustered into service: February 27, 1865
Date mustered out of service: January 31, 1866

Private Zacharias Garreth
Age: 31   Place of Birth\Residence: Adams County, Pa.
Occupation: Shoemaker
Date mustered into service: February 27, 1865
Date mustered out of service: January 31, 1866

Private Christian Hoover
Age: 28   Place of Birth\Residence: Lancaster County, Pa.
Occupation: Laborer
Date mustered into service: February 28, 1865
Deserted June 8, 1865

Private John S. Kauffman
Age: 27   Place of Birth\Residence: Lancaster County, Pa.
Occupation: Laborer
Date mustered into service: February 28, 1865
Date mustered out of service: January 31, 1866

Private Henry King
Age: 37   Place of Birth\Residence: York County, Pa.
Occupation: Laborer
Date mustered into service: February 27, 1865
Deserted November 20, 1865

Private Joseph A. Markley
Age: 34   Place of Birth\Residence: Chester County, Pa.
Occupation: Laborer
Date mustered into service: March 2, 1865
Date mustered out of service: January 31, 1866

Private Benjamin K. Minich
Age: 25   Place of Birth\Residence: Lancaster County, Pa.
Occupation: Miller
Date mustered into service: March 3, 1865
Date mustered out of service: January 31, 1866

Private John Myers

Age: 44   Place of Birth\Residence: York County, Pa.
Occupation: Laborer
Date mustered into service: February 23, 1865
Date mustered out of service: January 31, 1866

Private Ham Ney

Age: 20   Place of Birth\Residence: Lebanon County, Pa.
Occupation: Laborer
Date mustered into service: February 28, 1865
Deserted November 20, 1865

Private Jefferson Reaser

Age: 24   Place of Birth\Residence: Lancaster County, Pa.
Occupation: Coachmaker
Date mustered into service: February 25, 1865
Deserted August 13, 1865

Private Henry B. Seachrist

Age: 23   Place of Birth\Residence: York County, Pa.
Occupation: Farmer
Date mustered into service: March 7, 1865
Deserted June 29, 1865

Private Isaac Sensenig

Age: 18   Place of Birth\Residence: Lancaster County, Pa.
Occupation: Farmer
Date mustered into service: March 7, 1865
Deserted November 20, 1865

Private Jacob Sides

Age: 26   Place of Birth\Residence: Lancaster County, Pa.
Occupation: Shoemaker
Date mustered into service: February 27, 1865
Date mustered out of service: January 31, 1865

Private John Weaver

Age: 31   Place of Birth\Residence: Lancaster County, Pa.
Occupation: Laborer
Date mustered into service: February 28, 1865
Date mustered out of service: January 31, 1866

Private Thomas B. Walton

Age: 24   Place of Birth\Residence: York County, Pa.;
Lancaster County, Pa.

Occupation: Shoemaker

Date mustered into service: March 2, 1865

Date mustered out of service: January 31, 1866

Appendix II

Company H, 195th Pennsylvania Infantry: Desertions By Month

The following list is taken from Samuel P. Bates' *History of the Pennsylvania Volunteers 1861-1865*.

June:

6	–	Private Aug Rodewick
8	–	Private John Fox
"	–	Private William H. Hair
"	–	Private John Hicks
"	–	Private Christian Hoover
29	–	Private Samuel K. Able
"	–	Private Henry Dimler
"	–	Private Henry Seachrist

July: (None)

August:

5	–	Private William Matthias
6	–	Private Jeremiah Dimler
13	–	Sergeant Abraham Trostel
"	–	Private Jefferson Reaser

September:

13	–	Sergeant William H. Houseal

October:
   13 –   Sergeant Jacob List

November:
    8 –   Private John M. Ebersole
   16 –   Sergeant Reuben G. Sherman
   17 –   Private Jacob B. Burger
   20 –   Private John Colbough
   "   –   Private Miller M. Gable
   "   –   Private John Heisel
   "   –   Private Henry King
   "   –   Private William Knaub
   "   –   Private John Ney
   "   –   Private Ham Ney
   "   –   Private John Shullow
   21 –   Private Jacob Barnes
   "   –   Private Henry Dobbins
   "   –   Private David Eshelman
   "   –   Private Isaac C. Nelson
   "   –   Private David Sides
   23 –   Private Albert Frankhouser
   "   –   Private Henry Leas Jr.
   "   –   Private Charles Lockard
   "   –   Private Solomon Wambaugh

Obituaries of Thomas Beck Walton

Though taken from local newspapers, neither of the following accounts of Walton's life is completely accurate. There are errors in the date of Walton's marriage, as well as in the record of military service by Walton's brothers Amos George and Frank.

Huntingdon, Pennsylvania *Daily New Era*, November 28, 1913:

Thomas Beck Walton aged 73 years died at his home, 1203 Mifflin street yesterday morning, at 5:30 o'clock of heart failure.

Mr. Walton, who was the son of Hiram and Mary Walton, deceased was born in Holland, York County, Pa. In 1862 he married Emma M. Nophsker, who has been dead several years. In 1879 he came to Huntingdon and engaged in the general merchandise business, in Mifflin street, which he conducted in the present location until his death yesterday.

Mr. Walton served in the Civil War in company with his three brothers, Joseph, who resides in York, and Frank and Amos, who were killed in battle, all in one company: Company H, 195th regiment, Pennsylvania volunteers, second brigade, third divisions army of the Shenandoah.

For the past three years Mr. Walton has been afflicted with a weak heart. Three weeks ago it became so bad as to keep him in bed for part of the time since. Yesterday morning he arose about 5 o'clock and dressed. Half an hour later he died while sitting in a chair.

He is survived by two children, Thomas R. Walton, of 1129 Moore street, a clerk in the general offices of the Huntingdon and Broad Top Mountain Railroad and H. W. Walton, a druggist of Baltimore, Md. and his brother Joseph of York. H. Randolph Walton of this place, his grandson, was connected with him in his business.

The funeral will be held from the home of Thomas R. Walton, 1129 Moore Street, on Sunday at 2 p.m., and will be conducted by the George Simpson Post, No. 44, Grand Army of the Republic of which he was a member. The Rev. C. W. Sheriff, pastor of the Baptist church will officiate.

**Huntingdon, Pennsylvania *Semi-Weekly News,*
December 1, 1913:**

Thomas Beck Walton, for the past thirty-four years a merchant in Huntingdon and highly respected citizen, died suddenly of heart disease on Thursday morning, shortly after 5 o'clock at his home, 1203 Mifflin street. He became subject to heart attacks about three years ago, but previous to that time, for forty years he had never needed the attention of a physician, being in the best of health.

Mr. Walton was the son of Hiram and Mary Walton and was born at Holland, York county, Pa. on August 11, 1840. At the time of his death he was aged 73 years, three months and sixteen days. He was a shoemaker by trade, learning it at Middletown, Pa. and working at it there until 1869. He was united in marriage to Miss Emma M. Nophsker, of Bainbridge, Lancaster county, Pa., in 1869, and in the same years he went into the shoemaking business for himself at that place, with three men employed besides himself. His health failed, however, and he moved to Atkinsons Mills, Mifflin county, where he remained until the fall of 1879, when he moved to Huntingdon, and entered into the mercantile business. He remained in this business until his death, being assisted for the past few years by his grandson, H. Randolph Walton.

Mr. Walton was a veteran of the Civil War, having enlisted in Co. H., 195th Regiment, Pennsylvania Volunteers, serving with the Army of the Shenandoah. There were four brothers in the army, Amos, Frank, Joseph and T. B. Walton. Two of them were killed, Amos and Frank Walton. One of the brothers still lives, Joseph Walton, of York, Pa.

Mr. Walton was a member of the First Baptist Church of this place, and had been ever since he lived in Huntingdon. He was also a member of George Simpson Post No. 44, of this place. He was one of Huntingdon's most highly respected men, having the entire confidence and esteem of all who had dealings with him. He was a good man in every way – a real Christian gentleman.

His wife died on April 6, 1906, over seven years ago. He is survived by two sons – Howard W. Walton, a druggist at Baltimore, Md., and Thomas R. Walton, clerk in the H. & B. T. general office, Huntingdon. His grandson who has been associated with him in business for the past few years, H. Randolph Walton, will mourn him as a benefactor and protector in his early youth.

The funeral took place on Sunday afternoon from the residence of his son, Thomas R. Walton, 1129 Moore street. The services were conducted by his pastor, Rev. C. W. Sheriff, and the funeral was attended in a body by his old comrades, the members of Post 44, G.A.R. of this place, as well as by many friends and relatives. Interment in Riverview cemetery.

Notes

Introduction

1. Huntingdon *Semi-Weekly News*, December 1, 1912; and *Biographical Annals of Lancaster County Pennsylvania*, 4 vols. (1903, reprint edition, Spartanburg, S.C.: Reprint Co., 1985), vol. 2, p. 765.

2. Allen D. Albert, ed. *History of the Forty-Fifth Regiment Pennsylvania Veteran Volunteer Infantry, 1861-1865* (Williamsport, Pa.: Great Publishing Co., 1912), pp. 16, 23, 42-43.

3. U.S. Bureau of Census. *Population Schedules of the Eighth Census of the United States, 1860* (Washington, D.C.: National Archives, 1967), Roll 1124, Lancaster County, p. 203.

4. Albert, ed. *History of the Forty-Fifth Regiment*, pp. 54, 251.

5. John Gibson, ed. *History of York County Pennsylvania* (Chicago: F. A. Battery Publishing, 1886), p. 618.

6. Albert, ed. *History of the Forty-Fifth Regiment*, pp. 112, 136, 376.

7. William J. Miller. *The Training of An Army: Camp Curtin and the North's Civil War* (Shippensburg, Pa.: White Mane Publishing, 1990), p. 270.

8. Alex Haris. *Biographical History of Lancaster County, Pennsylvania* (1872, reprint ed. Baltimore, Md.: Genealogical Publishing Co., 1992), pp. 203-206. See also U.S. War Department. *War of the Rebellion: A Compilation of the Records of the Union and Confederate Armies,* 128 vols. (Washington, D.C.: Government Printing Office, 1880-1901). Series I, vol. 43, part 3, pp. 390-391, 442. Part 1, p. 765 (Hereinafter cited as *O.R.*); and Samuel P. Bates, *History of the Pennsylvania Volunteers*, 5 vols. (Harrisburg, Pa.: B. Singerly, 1871), vol. 5, p. 405.

9. *O.R.*, Series I, vol. 43, part 2, p. 509; and Bates, *History of the Pennsylvania Volunteers*, vol. 5, p. 405.

10. Richard A. Sauers. *Advance the Colors! Pennsylvania Civil War Battle Flags* (Harrisburg, Pa.: Capitol Preservation Committee, 1987-1991), vol. 1, p. 288.

11. Service Record, Pvt. Thomas B. Walton , Company H, 195th Pennsylvania Volunteer Infantry, Military Reference Branch, Military Archives Division, National Archives, Washington, D.C.; and *O.R.*, Series III, vol. 5, pp. 855-856. See also Fawn M. Brodie, *Thaddeus Stevens: Scourge of the South* (New York: Norton, 1959), pp. 96-97.

12. U.S. War Department, Adjutant-General's Office, Regimental Order Book, 195th Pennsylvania Volunteer Infantry, Record Group 94, National Archives, Washington D.C., March 12, 1865 (Hereinafter cited as Regimental Order Book).

13. Regimental Order Book, March 24, 1865.

14. *O.R.*, Series I, vol. 43, part 2, p. 529.

15. Regimental Order Book, January 26, 1866.

16. Huntingdon *Semi-Weekly News*, December 1, 1913.

17. Huntington *Semi-Weekly News*, January 13, 1913, and December 1, 1913.

The Civil War Diary of Thomas Beck Walton

1. Camp Cadwalader, located on Ishington Lane east of Ridge Road, was the primary collection point for recruits forming into units in Philadelphia. By 1865 the camp was at times over-crowded and the source of many complaints from soldiers housed there. See Frank H. Taylor, *Philadelphia in the Civil War* (Philadelphia, Pa.: By the City, 1913), p. 300.

2. Capt. Styer was a Lancaster County resident who mustered into service with the 195th Pennsylvania on March 16, 1865. See Samuel P. Bates, *History of the Pennsylvania Volunteers*, 5 vols. (Harrisburg, Pa.: B. Singerly, 1871), vol. 5, p. 300.

3. The 195th Pennsylvania was originally equipped with .58 caliber Springfield rifled muskets, the most common weapon used by Union troops. See Patricia Faust, ed. *Historical Times Illustrated Encyclopedia of the Civil War* (New York: Harper and Row, 1986), p. 710.

4. Chaplain William C. Walker of the 18th Connecticut Infantry, camped near Martinsburg, wrote that "March 23rd was a very cold, blustery day... In the afternoon at battalion drill there was a tremendous shower of rain and hail which forced the regiment back to camp in a hurry." See William C. Walker, *History of the Eighteenth Connecticut Volunteers...* (Norwich, Conn.: The Committee, 1885), p. 330.

5. Mosby's famed Confederate Rangers had recently clashed in nearby Loudoun County, Virginia with Federal cavalry and infantry, explaining the nervousness about a possible attack on 195th Pennsylvania positions. See Jeffry D. Wert, *Mosby's Rangers* (New York: Simon and Schuster, 1990), pp. 275-276.

6. The 195th Pennsylvania was brigaded with the 192nd Pennsylvania, 214th Pennsylvania, and the 192nd New York Infantry. See U.S. War Department, *War of the Rebellion: A Compilation of the Records of the Union and Confederate Armies*, 128 vols. (Washington, D.C.: Government Printing Office, 1880-1901), Series I, vol. 46, part 3, p. 1047 (Hereinafter cited as *O.R.*).

7. Near Petersburg, Lt. Col. Elisha Hunt Rhodes of the 2nd Rhode Island Infantry recorded in his diary that day, "Richmond has been evacuated and is in flames. Well let it burn, we do not want it. We are after Lee, and we are going to have him." See Robert Hunt Rhodes, ed. *All For the Union: The Civil War Diary and Letters of Elisha Hunt Rhodes* (New York: Vintage Civil War Library edition, 1992), p. 219.

8. One of Thomas B. Walton's surviving brothers, David Walton was a 29-year-old laborer from Conoy Township. See U.S. Bureau of Census, *Population Schedules of the Eighth Census of the United States, 1860* (Washington, D.C.: National Archives, 1967), Roll 1124, Lancaster County, p. 172 (Hereinafter cited as *Population Schedules*).

9. This is a probable reference to the battle fought at Sayler's Creek on April 6, 1865. There the retreating columns of the Army of Northern Virginia were badly mauled by Union forces commanded by Gen. Sheridan, losing some 8,000 men as prisoners. See. E. B. Long, *The Civil War Day By Day: An Almanac 1861-1865* (Garden City, N.Y.: Doubleday, 1971), pp. 667-668.

10. The United States Christian Commission was a civilian agency founded by the Y.M.C.A. in 1861 to look after the physical and spiritual well-being of Union soldiers in the field. One of its agents once wrote: "while caring for the body and laboring to alleviate bodily sufferings, we have aimed to lose no opportunity to speak a word for Jesus." The Winchester-Stevenson's Station area was supervised by Rev. N. C. Brackett as

Field Agent. See U.S. Christian Commission, *U.S. Christian Commission For the Army and Navy For the Year 1864. Third Annual Report* (Philadelphia, Pa.: James B. Rodgers Co., 1865), p. 85.

11. On April 9, 1865 the War Department ordered "a salute of 200 guns be fired at the headquarters of every army and department, every post and arsenal in the United States to celebrate Lee's surrender." See *O.R.*, Series I, vol. 46, part 3, pp. 683, 702.

12. Frederick M. Gramm was a 33-year-old boatman from Conoy Township. See *Population Schedules*, Roll 1124, Lancaster County, p. 212.

13. The order to suspend this movement came from Brig. Gen. Charles H. Morgan at Winchester. See *O.R.*, Series I, vol. 46, part 3, p. 774.

14. On April 16, 1865 the War Department officially announced to the Union armies "the untimely and lamentable death of the illustrious Abraham Lincoln, late President of the United States." See *O.R.*, Series I, vol. 46, part 3, p. 788.

15. The Christian Commission routinely supplied soldiers with free stationery and stamps to encourage letter-writing to family and friends at home. See James I. Robertson, Jr., *Soldiers Blue and Grey* (Columbia: University of South Carolina Press, 1988), p. 184.

16. A possible reference to Pvt. William McFeeters, Company C, 102nd Pennsylvania Infantry.

17. On April 23, 1865 Lt. Col. Bear appointed Pvt. Rusk K. Killam of Company H as the 195th's regimental postmaster. See U.S. War Department, Adjutant General's Office, Regimental Order Book, 195th Pennsylvania Volunteer Infantry, Record Group 94, National Archives, Washington, D.C., April 23, 1865 (Hereinafter cited as Regimental Order Book).

18. Division commander Maj. Gen. Thomas W. Egan on April 3, 1865 ordered all the regiments under his command to hold regular target practice at least three times per week to sharpen recent recruits' skills with their rifles. Firing was to take place between 11:00 AM and noon, with each soldier allotted 20 rounds of ammunition for this purpose. See Regimental Order Book, April 3, 1865.

19. Gen. Johnston and Maj. Gen. William T. Sherman had actually agreed to final surrender terms of all Confederate forces under Johnston's command on April 26, 1865. See Joseph E. Johnston, *Narrative of Military Operations During the Late War Between the States* (New York: 1874, reprint edition, Bloomington: Indiana University Press, 1959), pp. 412-414.

20. Brig. Gen. Green B. Raum, an Illinois native, saw considerable action at Vicksburg, Missionary Ridge, and during the Atlanta campaign. Contrary to the impression given in Ezra J. Warner's entry on Raum in his *Generals in Blue*, he not only commanded the 2nd Brigade, 3rd Provisional Division, Army of the Shenandoah, but served as a division commander also at times. Raum's resignation became official on May 6, 1865. See Warner, *Generals In Blue: Lives of the Union Commanders* (Baton Rouge: Louisiana State University Press, 1964), p. 791, and *O.R.*, Series I, vol. 46, part 3, pp. 774, 904, 1047.

21. Brig. Gen. Thomas H. Neill, born in Pennsylvania, was an 1847 graduate of West Point. According to Warner's *Generals In Blue* in 1864 "he joined Philip S. Sheridan in the Shenandoah early in September, serving as acting inspector general on the latter's staff until December after which he seems to have been unemployed." His inspection of the 195th Pennsylvania on May 12, 1865 clearly shows he continued in his inspector general's duties well into that year. See Warner, *Generals In Blue*, p. 343.

22. A sink was a Civil War era latrine trench measuring some 30 feet in length and 3 feet in depth. Diarrhea was doubtlessly the most common physical ailment afflicting both Union and Confederate soldiers. See Robertson, *Soldiers Blue and Grey*, pp. 151-152.

23. Dr. Z. Ring Jones was the 195th Pennsylvania's surgeon, having previously served in the 6th Pennsylvania Reserves and the 63rd Pennsylvania Infantry. Assistant Surgeon Harrison T. Whitman, a Berks County resident, also had experience from a tour with the 5th Pennsylvania Reserves. See Pennsylvania Adjutant General's Office, *Annual Report of the Adjutant General of Pennsylvania ... for the Year 1866* (Harrisburg, Pa.: Singerly and Myers, State Printers, 1867), p. 940; and Ira M. Rutkow, ed., *List of Battles and Roster of All Regimental Surgeons and Assistant Surgeons in the Late War Hospital Service* (Washington, D.C.: 1883, reprint edition, San Francisco: Novan Publishing, 1990), p. 204.

24. Company H's musicians were Privates Barnet Garreth, William Bensinger, and Frank G. Gailbraith. See Bates, *History of the Pennsylvania Volunteers*, vol. 5, p. 430.

25. Lt. Col. William L. Bear of Lancaster County was a veteran of the 1st Pennsylvania Reserves and fought at South Mountain in 1862. He joined the 195th Pennsylvania on March 12, 1865. Also, June 1 was a national day of prayer in memory of the murdered president. See *O.R.*, Series I, vol. 51, part 2, p. 142.

26. The "old" companies were A, B, and C, each composed of men from the 100-day version of the 195th who re-enlisted for one year's service in November, 1864. They were mustered out at Summit Point on June 21, 1865. See Bates, *History of the Pennsylvania Volunteers*, vol. 5, pp. 419-423.

27. For more on the various spellings of places along Walton's line of march in the Shenandoah Valley see John W. Wayland, *A History of Shenandoah County, Virginia* (1927, reprint edition. Baltimore: Regional Publishing Co., 1989), pp. 40, 143.

28. Hawkinstown was indeed known as an area with a number of old farms and homesteads. See Wayland, *Shenandoah*, p. 458.

29. Maj. Henry D. Markley led the 3 company battalion of the 195th to Staunton. See Bates, *History of the Pennsylvania Volunteers*, vol. 5, p. 404.

30. Lt. Col. Bear issued General Order No. 19 on this date concerning the 195th's relationship with the people of Harrisonburg. Soldiers could go to town on pass at 9:00 AM and 2:00 PM each day, but no man was allowed to remain there after dark. See Regimental Order Book, June 15, 1865.

31. Command of Company H went to Capt. William D. Stauffer, formerly a first lieutenant in Company C. He had also served in Company G of the 100-days regiment. See Bates, *History of the Pennsylvania Volunteers*, vol. 5, pp. 422, 429.

32. Bridgewater was located south of town on the Warm Springs and Harrisonburg Turnpike. See John W. Wayland, *A History of Rockingham County, Virginia* (1912, reprint edition, Harrisburg, Pa.: C. J. Carrier Co., 1980), p. 198.

33. Maj. Markley was from Berks County and had served as a captain in Company A in the 100-days regiment. He was promoted on February 27, 1865 and would stay in the army until discharged on March 22, 1866. See Bates, *History of the Pennsylvania Volunteers*, vol. 5, p. 419.

34. The 12th Pennsylvania Cavalry, commanded by Maj. Edison Gerry, was discharged on June 20, 1865. Its Companies E and F were raised in Lancaster County. See *O.R.*, Series I, vol. 46, part 3, p. 1048; and Richard A. Sauers, *Advance the Colors! Pennsylvania Civil War Battle Flags*, 2 vols. (Harrisburg, Pa.: Capitol Preservation Committee, 1987-1991), vol. 1, p. 272.

35. On December 8, 1863 Lincoln issued a proclamation of amnesty as part of his general plan to reconstruct the Union after final Confederate defeat. Most Southerners could be granted such an amnesty and pardon after taking an oath of allegiance to the United States. See James M. McPherson, *Battle Cry of Freedom: The Civil War Era* (New York: Oxford University Press, 1988), pp. 698-699.

36. A "French" furlough or leave was a Civil War slang expression for being absent without leave. See Bell I. Wiley, *The Life of Billy Yank* (Baton Rouge: Louisiana State University Press edition, 1978), p. 197.

37. The only possibilities are Privates Amos Benedick. Archibald Beatty, Joseph Markley, or John Myers. See Bates, *History of the Pennsylvania Volunteers*, vol. 5, p. 430.

38. Pvt. John Snearer died near Strasburg on July 28, 1865. See Bates, *History of the Pennsylvania Volunteers*, vol. 5, p. 429.

39. The Soldiers's Retreat was a mess hall near the railroad depot on New Jersey Avenue. See Margaret Leech, *Reveille In Washington* (New York: Harper and Brothers, 1941), p. 172.

40. Washington's street cars ran from Georgetown down Pennsylvania Avenue to the train depot and the Navy Yard. See Leech, *Reveille In Washington*, pp. 182-183.

41. Accoutrements were parts of a soldier's equipment such as a cartridge box or a canteen. See Mark M. Boatner III, *The Civil War Dictionary* (New York: Vintage Civil War Library edition, 1991), p. 2.

42. Smith was a 43-year-old Conoy Township resident who was involved in the lumbering business. See *Population Schedules*, Roll 1124, Lancaster County, p. 173.

43. The 195th Pennsylvania had a brigade inspection on this date at 6:00 AM. See Regimental Order Book, August 18, 1865.

44. Cpl. Beane was a Conoy Township native who previously served in Company C of the 100-days regiment. See Bates, *History of the Pennsylvania Volunteers*, vol. 5, p. 409.

45. Cpl. Benjamin F. Shoemaker of Company I would be found guilty of this offense by a court-martial board on September 12, 1865 and fined one month's pay. See Regimental Order Book, September 12, 1865.

46. Regimental Order Book, August 30, 1865.

47. On August 31, 1865, ten soldiers of Company I refused to stand guard duty at 17th and I Streets and were charged with attempting to "incite

and promote a mutiny, refusing to do duty as guards they being regularly detailed for that purpose." All were court-martialed and received six months at hard labor and in some cases dishonorable discharges. They were:

Private Horace C. Green

    "   Henry D. Hurst

    "   Philip McKim

    "   Daniel W. Kending

    "   Joseph McCormick

    "   Mathias Peters

    "   David Gilberson

    "   Nicholas Wolf

    "   Elias Miller

    "   Harvey S. Gehr

See Regimental Order Book, August 31, 1865.

48. Capt. Wallings commanded Company K, having previously served as a private in Company D and as commissary sergeant in the 100-days regiment. See Bates. *History of the Pennsylvania Volunteers*, vol. 5, pp. 406, 411, 432.

49. The Paymaster General's office was located in a large five-story house on the corner of 15th and F Streets. See Leech, *Reveille In Washington*, p. 228.

50. Grant had just returned from a trip to his boyhood home in Ohio. In a letter to Elihu B. Washburne dated October 8, 1865 he stated that he returned to Washington on October 7. However, in *The Papers of Ulysses S. Grant* a note reports that the general arrived on October 6. See John Y. Simon, ed. *The Papers of Ulysses S. Grant*, 15 vols. (Carbondale, Ill.: Southern Illinois University Press, 1988-), vol. 15, Grant to E. B. Washburne, October 10, 1865; and William S. McFeely, *Grant: A Biography* (New York: Norton, 1981), pp. 237-238.

51. Wolf's Station, or Mount Wolf, was a stop on the Northern Central Railroad some seven miles from York. See John Gibson, ed. *History of York County, Pennsylvania* (Chicago: F. A. Battery Publishing, 1886), p. 618.

52. The 194th Ohio Infantry, led by Col. Obadiah C. Maxwell, was organized in March, 1865. It was part of the 1st Brigade, 3rd Provisional

Division, Army of the Shenandoah until its transfer to Washington, D.C. in April. During its service it lost 38 enlisted men to disease. See *O.R.*, Series I, vol. 46, part 3, p. 1047; and Frederick A. Dyer. *A Compendium of the War of the Rebellion,* 3 vols. (1908, reprint edition, New York: Yoseloff, 1959), vol. 3, p. 1555.

53. Wirtz, former commander of the infamous Andersonville prison in Georgia, was sentenced in 1865 to hang for his role in the deaths of thousands of Union prisoners of war in his charge. His execution took place at 10:32 AM at the Old Capitol Prison yard before a large crowd, many of whom shouted "Down with him! Let him drop!" See A. A. Hoehling, *After the Guns fell Silent: A Post-Appomattox Narrative April 1865-March 1866* (Lanham, Maryland: Madison Books, 1990), p. 165.

54. Regimental Order Book, November 26, 1865.

55. Regimental Order Book, November 30, 1865.

56. The 214th Pennsylvania Infantry, under Col. David B. McKibbin, was brigaded with the 195th after its organization in March, 1865. It remained in Washington till it mustered out on March 21, 1866. Its Company B was raised in Lancaster County. See Sauers, *Advance the Colors*, vol. 1, p. 300; *O.R.*, Series I, vol. 46, part 3, p. 1047; and Dyer, *A Compendium*, vol. 3, p. 1563.

57. On mustering out, Walton received $26.22 due on his clothing account and $66.00 in remaining bounty money owed him. See Service Record, Pvt. Thomas B. Walton, Company H, 195th Pennsylvania Infantry, Military Reference Branch, Military Archives Division, National Archives, Washington, D.C.

Bibliography

Albert, Allen D., ed. *History of the Forty-Fifth Regiment Pennsylvania Veteran Volunteer Infantry 1861-1865*. Williamsport, Pa.: Great Publishing Co., 1912.

Bates, Samuel P. *History of the Pennsylvania Volunteers*, 5 vols., Harrisburg, Pa.: B. Singerly. 1871.

Biographical Annals of Lancaster County, Pennsylvania. 4 vols., 1903, reprint edition, Spartanburg, S.C.: Reprint Co., 1985.

Boatner, Mark M. III. *The Civil War Dictionary*. New York: Vintage Civil War Library edition, 1991.

Brodie, Fawn. *Thaddeus Stevens: Scourge of the South*. New York: Norton, 1959.

Dyer, Frederick A. *A Compendium of the War of the Rebellion*. 3 vols., 1908, reprint edition, New York: Yoseloff, 1959.

Faust, Patricia, ed. *Historical Times Illustrated Encyclopedia of the Civil War*. New York: Harper and Row, 1986.

Gibson, John, ed. *History of York County, Pennsylvania*. Chicago: F. A. Battery Publishing, 1886.

Harris, Alex. *Biographical History of Lancaster County, Pennsylvania*. 1872, reprint edition, Baltimore, Md.: Genealogical Publishing Co., 1992.

Hoehling, A. A. *After the Guns Fell Silent: A Post-Appomattox Narrative April 1865-March 1866*. Lanham, Md.: Madison Books, 1990.

Huntingdon (Pa.), *Daily New Era*.

Huntingdon (Pa.), *Semi-Weekly News*.

Johnston, Joseph E. *Narrative of Military Operations During the Late War Between the States*. 1874, reprint edition, Bloomington: Indiana University Press, 1959.

Leech, Margaret. *Reveille In Washington*. New York: Harper and Brothers, 1941.

Long, E. B. *The Civil War Day By Day: An Almanac 1861-1865*. Garden City, N.J.: Doubleday, 1971.

McFeely, William S. *Grant: A Biography.* New York: Norton, 1981.

McPherson, James M. *Battle Cry of Freedom: The Civil War Era*. New York: Oxford University Press, 1988.

Miller, William J. *The Training of An Army: Camp Curtin and the North's Civil War*. Shippensburg, Pa.: White Mane Publishing Co., 1990.

Pennsylvania Adjutant General's Office. *Annual Report of the Adjutant General of Pennsylvania...for the Year 1866*. Harrisburg. Pa.: Singerly and Myers, State Printers, 1867.

Rhodes, Robert Hunt, ed. *All for the Union: The Civil War Diary and Letters of Elisha Hunt Rhodes*. New York: Vintage Civil War Library edition, 1992.

Robertson, James I., Jr. *Soldiers Blue and Grey*. Columbia: University of South Carolina Press, 1988.

Rutkow, Ira M., ed. *List of Battles and Roster of All Regimental Surgeons and Assistant Surgeons in the Late War Hospital Service*. 1883. reprint edition. San Francisco: Novan Publishing. 1990.

Sauers. Richard A. *Advance the Colors! Pennsylvania Battle* Flags. 2 vols. Harrisburg, Pa.: Capitol Preservation Committee, 1987-1991.

Simon, John Y., ed. *The Papers of Ulysses S. Grant*. 15 vols., Carbondale, Ill.: Southern Illinois University Press, 1988- .

Taylor, Frank H. *Philadelphia in the Civil War*. Philadelphia, Pa.: By the City, 1913.

U.S. Bureau of Census. *Population Schedules of the Eighth Census of the United States, 1860*. Washington, D.C.: National Archives, 1967, Roll 1124, Lancaster County, Pa.

U.S. Christian Commission. *U.S. Christian Commission For the Army and Navy for the Year 1864, Third Annual Report*. Philadelphia, Pa.: James B. Rodgers Co., 1865.

U.S. War Department. Adjutant General's Office. Regimental Order Book, 195th Pennsylvania Volunteer Infantry, Record Group 94, National Archives, Washington, D.C.

———. *War of the Rebellion: A Compilation of the Records of the Union and Confederate Armies*. 128 vols., Washington, D.C.: Government Printing Office, 1880-1901.

Walker, William C. *History of the Eighteenth Connecticut Volunteers....* Norwich, Conn.: The Committee, 1885.

Walton, Thomas Beck. Private, Company H, 195th Pennsylvania Volunteer Infantry. Service Record, Military Reference Branch, Military Archives Division, National Archives, Washington, D.C.

Warner, Ezra J. *Generals In Blue: Lives of the Union Commanders*. Baton Rouge: Louisiana State University Press, 1964.

Wayland, John W. *A History of Shenandoah County, Virginia*. 1927, reprint edition, Baltimore, Md.: Regional Publishing Co., 1989.

———. *A History of Rockingham County, Virginia*. 1912, reprint edition, Harrisburg, Pa.: C. J. Carrier Co., 1980.

Wert, Jeffry D. *Mosby's Rangers*. New York: Simon and Schuster, 1990.

Wiley, Bell I. *The Life of Billy Yank*. Baton Rouge: Louisiana State University Press edition, 1978.

Index